MW01061502

Tea in the City:

Paris

A tea lover's guide
to sipping and shopping
in the city

Jane Pettigrew
Bruce Richardson

TEA ROOMS TEA SHOPS TEA LOUNGES TEA SALONS
HOTEL TEAS CAFÉ TEAS MUSEUM TEAS

BENJAMIN PRESS
PO Box 100
Perryville, Kentucky 40468
800.765.2139
www.benjaminpress.com

ISBN 978-0-9793431-0-0
Printed in China through
Four Colour Imports

Cover photo: Angelina

Every effort has been made to guarantee the accuracy of listings
in this guidebook. But in a city known for fashionable innovation,
change is constant. Avoid disappointment by phoning to verify
information before setting out on the tea trail.

Tea in the City: Paris

A tea lover's guide
to sipping and shopping in the city

Seeing Paris with Tea on Your Mind

Paris is a city that never disappoints me. Every arrondissement is a treasure chest waiting to be opened, sniffed, consumed and remembered. I gaze longingly into boulangerie windows, wander through outdoor markets, and relish the daily menus hastily chalked onto boards posted outside cafés.

Fortunately, it's an easy city to walk. If you're like me, you'll need to burn off those decadent calories you consume while satisfying your hunger for the most delicious city in the world. The long climb up Montmartre from the Moulin Rouge to the cathedral Sacré Coeur is one of the best workouts for shedding those buttery excesses.

For those of us addicted to the leaf of the *Camellia sinensis*, the great consolation is that we are never more than a short stroll from a salon de thé! And there are all those enticing pâtisseries to be sampled...a gâteau of this, a tarte of that, a croissant with honey, another madeleine, a dozen boxed

> For those of us addicted to the leaf of the *Camellia sinensis*, the great consolation is that we are never more than a short stroll from a salon de thé!

meringues to take home, or a pain au chocolat to leave a sweet taste on the tongue. Why are these people so thin?

With their innate sense of style and creativity, the French have elevated the act of taking tea to a refined art form. They treat tea with the same respect and attention to detail they reserve for all endeavors, whether culinary, fashion, or the visual arts.

In this capital of sophistication, the ancient beverage is skillfully brewed and paired with foods that can only be described as "too beautiful to eat." The French understand better than anyone that presentation is as important as taste in the culinary world.

France was one of the first European countries

to adopt this Asian brew. Tea has never been as synonymous to French culture as it is to British routine. Tea in Great Britain is often taken for granted; the country has a set pattern for brewing a few well-known teas. But the French are more open to finding and embracing the best teas and tea traditions from around the world. Tea salons in Paris have some of the most complete tea menus to be found anywhere.

From Paris, I love to take easy day trips to Giverny, Chartres, or Versailles. Good tea can be had in all these locations along with a beautiful plate of fresh pastries or gâteaux. You may be tempted to give up scones forever!

My favorite Parisian museum is the Musée D'Orsay with its spectacular collection of impressionist paintings. Housed in a former train station, it is easy to navigate and much less crowded than the Louvre. Plus, it has a beautiful café where you can pause for a cup of tea and a plate of madeleines.

Whether you visit the Louvre or the D'Orsay, you're not far from one of Paris's oldest and best-known tea salons, Angelina. Since 1903, it has hosted such luminaries as Marcel Proust and Coco Chanel in an elegant setting. The interior is reminiscent of a gilded chocolate box, with its mirrored walls and gold piping, and the pale, lime green fabric lining all the shelves.

While visiting Notre Dame, I suggest you slip into a side street named *rue Saint-Louis-en-I'lle* for tea or chocolate at a charming little café run by a flamboyant woman of a certain age who could probably tell great stories of *la vie de bohème* after a carafe or two of wine. La Charlotte de L'isle is a cluttered little fairyland where the most requested cup contains what the *New York Times* calls "the absinthe of hot chocolate."

If you find yourself across the Seine from the Eiffel Tower, stop by Carette at Trocadero Place for a 1930's tea experience accompanied by freshly made madeleines or palmières in a relaxed atmosphere. Further west, near Place de Passy, is Thé Cool, a cozy neighborhood salon de thé offering tea in iron Asian pots accompanied by some of the most beautiful desserts you will find this side of Provence.

My other off-the-beat-en-path tea haunts are Les Nuits des Thés where the owner's dog greets you at the door and joins you at the table - if invited; Place Numéro Thé, run by a young woman who is passionate in her devotion to tea; Le Stübli, an Austrian bakery with a second floor tea salon and a colorful street market outside the front door; and A Priori Thé, housed under glass in the Galerie Vivienne, a nineteenth-century shopping arcade.

If it's a combination tea room and tea shop you desire, you can't beat Mariage Frères. With over 500 teas on the menu, this veteran world-class tea purveyor has three locations. Each has endless shelves of tea canisters and an interesting tea museum to keep you occupied while you wait for a table. Be assured, every pot will be perfectly brewed.

Other outstanding tea shops include Thés de Chine, known for puehrs and artisan teas; Lyne's, where you will find outstanding Taiwanese oolongs; and Thé O Dor, offering exotic blended and flavored teas in a fascinating shop that long ago housed a creamery. All are easily accessible via the safe and efficient Paris Metro.

The list that Jane and I have compiled in this guide goes on and on. Paris, like any delicacy, should be savored in petite bites so that you don't satiate your appetite. There will be more *salons de thé* during a future visit. They've been doing tea correctly here for 375 years, and you know it's only going to get better!

Easy Day Trips from Paris

Three glorious destinations lie within easy reach of Paris via train. Château de Versailles is mentioned in the final chapter of this book. Chartres and Giverny are the other gems that should not be missed. You may not be able to see them all on your first visit to Paris. Don't worry. Paris is a city that you will return to again and again.

Chartres Cathedral

Chartres

You leave the big city life of Paris far behind when you step onto the train platform in the medieval town of Chartres. The town is built around Europe's best example of a pure Gothic cathedral. Pilgrims have made their way here for almost a thousand years. Don't miss the labyrinth built into the floor as you enter. The windows contain one of world's largest collections of medieval glass from the 13th century. Three rose windows at the entrances come alive at different times through the day as the sun finds its way into this holy space.

The cobblestone streets are easy to walk and explore. Bakeries, tea rooms, gift shops and open markets await you nearby.

Monet's House at Giverny

Giverny

Claude Monet moved his family to the tiny village of Giverny, 50 miles northwest of Paris, in 1883 and established forever one of the best-known artists' retreats of the early 20th century.

His home and resplendent gardens are open to the public. The farmhouse and studio are as he left them - a colorful collage of green, blue, and yellow that found their way to his painter's palette. The gardens have been restored to resemble the colorful plan laid out by Monet over a hundred years ago. The famous lily pond, where he often enjoyed tea, still has the Japanese red bridge and row boat pictured in his paintings found in the Musée D'Orsay and L'Orangerie in Paris. The town is filled with artists' studios, boutique hotels, cafés and museums.

Exploring Paris:
A City of World Teas
and International
Culture

I first went to Paris as a teenager and felt overwhelmed by my decided lack of fluent French. There also was my sense of awe at the city's expensive shops, vast art galleries and museums, palaces, monuments, and architectural wonders. Despite the fact that I had grown up in London and was perfectly at ease with its busy streets, noisy traffic, and tall buildings, Paris seemed grander, more elegant and spacious with its wide boulevards and huge roundabouts, and perhaps more daunting with its hooting cars and seemingly hostile policemen.

As I grew up and became better acquainted with Paris, I gradually fell in love with its slightly dotty way of life in which gentility, refinement, high fashion, and stylish restaurants are somehow mixed up with student anger, a love of disruptive street demonstrations, and a sense of bohemian scruffiness left over from the 1960s and 70s. Today, I feel as much at home in Paris as I do in London, especially now that there are so many unusual, exciting, and beautiful places to go for tea.

My introduction to tea in Paris came in the early 1990s when Gilles Brochard, tea specialist, writer, and broadcaster (and now a great friend) invited me to speak at a meeting of the recently inaugurated *Club des Buveurs de Thé* – the French Tea Club. This also served as the foundation for my understanding of how our British national beverage was becoming equally important to some Parisians. During my visit, I was treated like a princess. I had flowers in my hotel room and a place of honor at the top table on the day of the tea event. I was whisked around Paris to eat in the best restaurants, met the top chocolatiers (who were using tea as an ingredient in their delicious confectionery long before we had even heard of the idea), and visited a few of the tea shops that had already been established.

Since then, Gilles and I have taken tea together many times. Whenever I go to Paris, he grabs me by the hand, and together

> I fell in love with the slightly dotty way of life in Paris, where gentility, refinement, high fashion, and stylish restaurants are somehow mixed up with student anger, a love of disruptive street demonstrations, and a sense of bohemian scruffiness left-over from the 1960s and 70s.

we jump on buses and dive down into the metro to go and see the latest tea salon or retail counter. We meet the latest tea entrepreneur who is setting up something new and explore the suburban back streets to enjoy the latest tea adventure. Gilles has introduced me to Japanese, Chinese, Vietnamese, Laotian, Greek, Taiwanese, American, and Egyptian tea proprietors – and of course many French ones, too – who are selling, brewing, and serving an amazing range of teas.

In Paris today, the selection of tea is outstanding, with some shops and tea rooms offering teas from just about every growing region or country in the world. The variety of tea rooms in the city reflects the mixture of influences

> In Paris today, the selection of tea is outstanding.... The variety of tea rooms in the city reflects the mixture of influences that make Paris so colorful and interesting.

that make Paris so colorful and interesting. Considering French colonial history in Indochina, it is not surprising to find so many Vietnamese and Chinese who have settled here. The Japanese seem to love the refined side of Paris life and have added their own style to create a fascinating fusion of Oriental and European design, tea, and food. There are Russian links too, still evident in names that date back to the days when influential Russians spoke French and spent as much time in Paris as they did in St. Petersburg and Moscow.

So when you visit Paris, don't expect to only drink tea French style. Explore the diversity of personality, the varying cultural influences, and the international flavor of tea in Paris.

A Luxurious Indulgence:
The Story of Tea in Paris

In the early part of the 17th century, long after tea had found its way from China to lands that stretched westward to the Baltic Sea and eastward to Korea and Japan, the beverage started to appear in Europe. The Dutch East India Company had established trading posts on the coast of China's southeastern provinces, and by 1610 the company was shipping quantities of both green and black tea home to Amsterdam.

Although *tea* in Mandarin is *cha*, the Amoy dialect for the beverage in the areas familiar to the Dutch traders was *te*. Thus, the Dutch early on learned to call this new herb *thee,* passing the name on to their customers in Europe. When the French discovered its delicious taste and refined character in the mid-1630s, they pronounced the name in the same way and transcribed it as *thé*. Eventually, the English adapted the word, changing the pronunciation and spelling to arrive at *tea*.

In France, as in other European countries of that era, tea became very popular in the grandest, wealthiest houses and was served in small porcelain bowls to important and aristocratic visitors. Although the French government did not impose as high a tax as did the English parliament, tea in the 17th century was a luxurious indulgence purchased in small quantities by royalty and the aristocracy and brewed as a special and rather exotic drink.

At court, tea drinking was so new and remarkable that aristocrat Madame de Sévigné, who recorded much that happened at court in regular letters to her daughter, mentioned it frequently. She described how the Princesse de Tarente drank twelve cups every day and how Madame de la Sablière added milk to her tea because that was how she liked it. Cardinal Mazarin, French chief minister from 1642 to 1661, apparently drank tea regularly, and King Louis XIV developed a liking for tea and drank it as a tonic beverage to protect against heart problems and gout. As in Britain some years later, early supplies of the dry leaf were available from apothecary shops, and the brew was taken as a healthy tonic rather than simply as an enjoyable refreshment.

Cardinal Mazarin, French chief minister from 1642 to 1661, apparently drank tea regularly, and King Louis XIV developed a liking for tea and drank it as a tonic beverage to protect against heart problems and gout.

More and more people took to the brew, and the French stopped relying on the Dutch for their supply, shipping their own chests from China along with exquisite silk, fine translucent porcelains, and precious stones. But although tea remained popular as a luxurious upper class indulgence, coffee and chocolate seemed to interest the French more and gradually took over as more commonly consumed beverages.

The social upheaval of the French Revolution dealt a blow to French tea drinking, at least temporarily. As the underprivileged, poorer classes grew more vocal and violent in their demands for equality and justice, so they turned against the wealthy whom they saw as self-serving and corrupt. Tea drinking – as a habit of the privileged few – was viewed as an indulgence to be eliminated.

Once the madness and social uproar was over and life resumed a more normal routine, new influences began to play their part. During the 1830s and 40s, at almost exactly the same time that the 7th Duchess of Bedford was indulging in private tea-drinking gatherings in the stately homes of England, many French citizens decided that everything English was to be the latest trend. This, of course, included tea drinking. Tea was served after dinner and, as tea accompanied by sweet indulgences became important to upper class society in England and North America, so the French followed

suit. Companies such as Limoges and Sèvres produced delicate teacups and saucers, teapots, sugar bowls, and an inventive warming stand called a *veilleuse* that looked rather like an ornate porcelain chimney with a small chamber for a candle beneath a stand on which the teapot could be kept warm.

As the fashion continued, tea companies were established in Paris and found regular customers for their loose leaf teas. Some still thrive today. Mariage Frères, perhaps the best-known, dates back to the late 17th century when Nicolas Mariage started trading tea. By the early part of the 19th century, a descendant of his, Jean-Francois Mariage, was still involved in the tea business. His two sons, Aimé and Auguste, set up Auguste Mariage & Compagnie in Paris in

1845, and the name later changed to Mariage Frères under Aimé's sons. The company still trades out of its original premises in rue du Bourg-Tibourg in the Marais district, owns three tea salons and retail shops in the center of Paris, and has outlets in several of the grand department stores.

Another venerable firm, Thé de l'Éléphant, was founded in 1897 and traded teas from China, India, and Ceylon until it was taken over

---

> Mariage Frères dates back to
> the late 17th century when Nicolas
> Mariage started trading tea....
> The company still trades
> out of its original premises in rue
> du Bourg-Tibourg in the Marais district.

---

by Lipton in 1968. Établissements George Cannon was established by an English teaman of that name in 1898, at the height of the craze for all things English. Dammann, another important name in Parisian tea history, was founded in 1925 and was chosen as the official tea supplier to the French Compagnie Génerale Transatlantique, whose customers sailed the high seas on such famous liners as the Normandie and the France.

Indar-Compagnie Coloniale is a combined enterprise of Indar, founded in 1887, and la Compagnie Coloniale, founded in 1848. Betjeman & Barton was set up by Irishman Arthur Betjeman in 1919 and the name continues today but under French ownership. All those established names may be found in the various food halls, department stores, and supermarkets alongside the more recently introduced companies such as Contes de Thés and L'Empire des Thés, and other internationally recognized companies such as Twinings, Lipton, and Taylors of Harrogate.

Since the 1960s, interest in tea has grown remarkably, and annual consumption has risen from 3,000 tons to approximately 15,000 tons today. In 1988, one in seven French consumers drank tea at breakfast time; today it is more than one in four. According to

surveys carried out in the last five years, 40 percent of French tea drinkers enjoy tea at breakfast, 60 percent drink it during the afternoon, and 30 percent indulge in the evening. Fifty-eight percent of all French people drink tea, and sixty-one percent of those drink it regularly. The French tea market is estimated to be worth approximately 122 million euros.

Despite the common roots, there are distinct differences between tea drinking in Britain and in France. The French tend to drink their teas much lighter and rarely add milk or sugar. The big international tea companies blend teas differently for the French market, aiming for less strength and more subtle flavor. The range that interests the French tea drinker tends to be more varied than in Britain. Perhaps because of France's past connections with Indochina, there is a taste for lighter Chinese blacks such as Keemun and Sichuan, and oolongs from the Chinese mainland and from Taiwan. Historical French links to Russian aristocracy mean that several companies also sell a Russian style black tea blend that has a slightly smoky character, replicating the early black teas that were transported overland into Russia.

Most tea lists in Paris include classic Darjeelings, Ceylons, large-leafed orthodox Assams, and teas with names such as Tea of the Buddha, Tibetan Secret, Marco Polo, and Babouchka that are flavored with exotic fruits and flowers and take you on a spiritual journey to far-flung lands. Green and white teas are becoming more and more popular, and one or two of the adventurous tea salons serve cocktails carefully balanced with a certain measure of particular teas.

There seems to be a greater understanding of good brewing practice than in London, a standard set perhaps by Mariage Frères, who have, for many years, been serving perfectly brewed liquor without the leaf strewn in the bottom of the teapot. Their well trained tea brewers work in a dedicated corner of each tea room to carefully weigh out the correct quantity of leaf, check the temperature of the water poured onto it, set a timer to the exact number of minutes and seconds required, and then decant the liquor into a warmed pot ready for the customer. Other tea salons use large paper filters, artistically tie a knot in the top of the bag and leave the customer to lift it from the pot onto a neat saucer or dish when the recommended number of minutes has passed. Some of the more traditional tea rooms still brew the loose leaf in the bottom of the pot and serve it to the table with a tea strainer, and some use teabags, although few brew with the paper variety, choosing instead prettier bags made of muslin, nylon gauze, or cotton gauze that allow the customer to enjoy the leaf visually as well as for its taste. I suspect that much of the brewing expertise has come from the intervention and charmingly persistent nagging of Gilles Brochard. Paris is lucky to have him teaching and advising, encouraging, and enthusing more and more people to offer excellent tea and brew it well.

It was Gilles and a group of friends and associates who had the idea in the late 1980s of forming a tea club. Although the Club des Buveurs de Thé no longer exists, it had a profound effect on Paris for approximately ten years through its presence and activities at some of the most stylish and revered hotels. Gilles and his co-directors went on to help similar groups of tea lovers in Belgium and Switzerland and even came to London for a shared tea party with the UK Tea Club before that too was sadly disbanded. His continuing mission and the work of a growing number of tea entrepreneurs has meant that there now is an exciting array of places in which to buy and take tea in Paris.

The French don't do Afternoon Tea in the way that the British or Americans do. The event is not bound by strict rules as to what should be served or eaten, and there is rarely a three-tier cake stand on the table except in the most expensive hotels. The way the French take their tea in the afternoon is to choose their preferred tea and then select food à la carte, which can mean nibbling on little canapés or other dainty savories, or enjoying slices of wonderful tarts and gâteaux, small Japanese sweetmeats called *wagashi*, or sponge cakes flavored with green tea. The French love their tiny little yo-yo macaroons that are more like melt-in-the-mouth meringues and come in all the colors and shades of a painter's palette. Talented pastry chefs blend flavors, colors, textures, and often different teas to create many other irresistibly beautiful confectionery with exotic, unusual tastes.

In the grand hotels of Paris, you may find the traditional full Afternoon Tea being offered with neat, crustless, English-style sand-

> The French love their tiny little yo-yo macaroons that are more like melt-in the-mouth meringues and come in all the colors and shades of a painter's palette.

wiches, warm scones and madeleines (those little, boat-shaped sponge cakes that Marcel Proust associated with past treasured moments), and delicate pâtisseries. These last are usually artistically arranged on a trolley or cake stand and will have you reaching for your camera to capture the sheer inventiveness of the display.

Styles vary from ultra-chic and streamlined to rococo ornateness. You can find palatial grandeur or French bohemian, the ambience of a traditional Chinese tea shop or the cottage style of an English country tea room.

But don't always expect clotted cream. Instead there may be a soft creamy mixture of mascarpone and crème frâiche served with fruity preserves and jellies flavored with tea.

As visitors wander around Paris, they see the words *salon de thé* inscribed on the windows or awnings of many restaurants. Beware! This does not automatically mean that you will be able to drink wonderful teas and eat typical tea-time foods. It simply means that if you ask for tea, you will get tea, but in many instances, it may be a nondescript, low-quality teabag in a pot or a cup. The tea rooms and salons worth patronizing often do not call themselves *salon de thé* but simply go by their established name – Angelina, Cador, Thés de Chine, L'Infinithé, Mariage Frères. This guide brings together the best in the center of Paris and its immediate suburbs, but there will undoubtedly be more by the time readers visit Paris. So before deciding to go in and settle at one of the tables inside any tea room not listed here, check the extent of the tea list, run your eyes over the counter and shelves to see how many tins of tea are on display, glance at other tables to see what sort of teapots are used and how the tea has been brewed and presented. If you see too familiar names on tags dangling from teabags that are washing around in cups, walk away. The variety of good tea rooms in this book mean that you will not have to go far to find something much, much better.

This collection offers a wide variety of tea experiences from China, Japan, Vietnam, England, Morocco, and France. Styles vary from ultra-chic and streamlined to rococo ornateness. You can find palatial grandeur or French bohemian, the ambience of a traditional Chinese tea shop or the cottage style of an English country tea room. I hope you will be charmed, inspired, delighted, and amazed at the journey on which these wonderful shops and tea rooms will take you.

15

Paris: Orientation 101

Navigating the streets of Paris can be daunting, even for natives of the city. Paris is divided into 20 arrondissements or neighborhoods. They spiral out from the area of the Louvre. To help you find that one special tea room - or a cluster of tea rooms in a particular district - *Tea in the City* features a map with color codes for the arrondissements grouped together in each section. The maps are not drawn to scale, and all designated boundaries are approximate. For more specific directions, each tea room entry includes a street address and travel recommendations. At the back of the book, you will find a comprehensive index of tea rooms, shopping venues, and historic sites.

Each listing includes a description of the tea room, hours of operation, street address, transportation tips, and cost rating based on Euros (E = inexpensive, EE = moderate, and EEE = expensive).

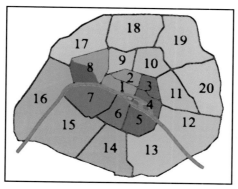

The map of central Paris (above) shows the general location of arrondissements cited in this guidebook. The standard French abbreviation for arrondissement is used throughout this book (1e, 2e, etc.).

Palaces and Royal Gardens (1e, 2e)

Notre Dame and Île. St. Louis (3e, 4e)

Latin Quarter (5e)

From St. Germain to Montparnasse (6e, 7e)

Empire and Republic (8e, western portions)

Madeleine (8e, eastern portions)

From New Athens to the Bastille (9e-13e)

The Eiffel Tower and Beyond (14e, 15e, 16e)

Northern Hills (17e, 18e, 19e)

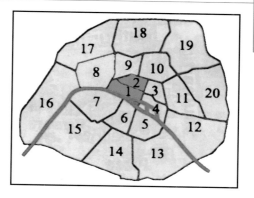

Palaces and Royal Gardens

Arrondissements 1, 2

On both sides of the sweep of land that runs from the western edges of the elegant Tuileries Gardens up the Rue de Rivoli to the Pont Neuf, you will find a fascinating cross-section of long established classic Parisian tea salons, Japanese tea rooms, Chinese tea retail stores, and elegant hotels where afternoon tea is a palatial indulgence.

Angelina

Arrondissement: 1e
226 rue de Rivoli, Paris 75001

With its red carpet and walls lined with vast gilded mirrors, Angelina has been an important part of Paris life since 1903. Its convenient location in the arcade opposite the Louvre makes it a favorite stopping off place for hot chocolate, coffee, and tea. This is an ideal place to purchase impressive cakes, delicious pastries, and fine chocolates to take home.

At the front of the shop, gleaming counters are laden with an eye-caching display of meringues, fruit tartlets, macaroons, mont-blanc meringues, mille feuilles slices, apricot tarts, pains aux raisins, and croissants. All are baked fresh throughout the day by four pastry chefs. If you have to wait for a table (normal at busy times) you will find it hard to decide which creation is most tempting. Beyond this

indulgence-packed section of the establishment, the vast salon opens up to accommodate around 150 customers in its palatial gold and cream grandeur. The vast dimensions of the Belle Epoque architecture are reflected in the huge mirrors on both sides of the room. Guests are seated around marble-topped tables, and waiters and waitresses clad in reassuring black and white uniforms deliver pots of tea, hot chocolate, cakes, and full platters of savory foods. The service is efficient but not overly friendly (although regulars are recognized and charmingly welcomed), and the atmosphere is busy, unfussy, a little matter-of-fact, and very French. Upstairs is a more intimate room with a lower ceiling and less gilt, used only when the downstairs is overflowing.

The loose leaf tea is brewed in silver teapots and served in traditional style without a tea strainer but with a pot of hot water. It's not outstanding but will satisfy while you sit and watch the Parisians at play. Choose from Angelina blend, Darjeeling, Ceylon, Earl Grey, China Lapsang Souchong, and green.

• Tea room and retail counter open Mon.-Fri. 8am-7pm, Sat.-Sun. 9am-7pm • Nearest metro: Tuileries (Line 1), Concorde (Lines 1, 8, 12) • Tel: 01 42 60 82 00 • Major credit cards • Breakfast, lunch, tea à la carte, pâtisserie, chocolates • E

Bar Vendôme - Hôtel Ritz Paris
Arrondissement: 1e
15 place Vendôme, Paris 75001

Although a very pleasing experience, afternoon tea at the Paris Ritz does not have as much glamour and cache as tea at the Ritz in London or at the George V or Le Bristol in Paris. The style is more traditional English than chic French, and the presentation is perhaps a little tired. Even so, the muted warm light of the lounge area sets a restful and calm ambience. Many people will enjoy taking tea in a room that has not changed for years, while contemplating the many historic connections that the hotel boasts. The décor is period style with thick carpets and rich purple velvet upholstery. In summer, when the weather allows, tea may be taken on the Italian patio, where statues and fountains, marble columns, white wrought-iron tables, and flowering shrubs set a Tuscan theme.

(Continued on page 22)

"Le Five O'clock at the Ritz Paris, an import from London, had swiftly become an institution; ladies of impeccable background were to be seen among the mirrors and flower arrangements of the salon de thé sipping tea from expensive porcelain and indulging in an occasional meringue or bonbon."

Mark Boxer
(Former editorial director of Condé Nast)

"Staff members are very friendly,
and the scones, cakes, desserts, and savory tarts
are delicious."

A Priori Thé
Arrondissement: 2e
35-37 Galerie Vivienne, Paris 75002

Galerie Vivienne is one of Paris' charming, Victorian arcades that are concealed behind grander buildings whose facades dominate the historic side streets. This passageway, with its high glass roof and stately arched entrances, guards its secrets closely, but if you take the time to wander in from rue Vivienne, rue de la Banque or rue des Petits Champs, you will find a quality wine merchant, chic clothing shops, and Peggy Hancock's lovely, English-style tea room.

As you turn into the arcade, you will see tables that stand outside the shop decked with pink cloths and fresh flowers, tempting you to stop awhile and take tea. The shop has a sort of student air about it with its wooden furniture, mixed clientele, and crowded, busy, take-us-as-we-are atmosphere. Staff members are very friendly, and the scones, cakes, desserts, and savory tarts are delicious. The teas (stored in tall, old-fashioned, japanned tins behind the counter) are well brewed in infuser baskets that customers can lift out when the tea is ready. Originally from America, Peggy herself sits behind a small table to the right of the counter. She adds up the bills, takes the money and, rather like a traditional concierge, keeps a watchful eye on the shop and her customers, many of whom visit regularly.

The long list of loose leaf teas includes several black teas from China, India, and Sri Lanka; greens and flavored greens from China, Japan and Vietnam; oolongs and souchongs from China and Taiwan; and plenty of flavored teas to choose from (almond, cinnamon, Old Autumn, chai with orange blossom honey, jasmine, caramel, vanilla), and a few herbals (mint, camomile, vanilla rooibos).

• Tea room open Mon.-Fri. 9am-6pm, Sat. 9am-6:30pm, Sun. 12:30-6:30pm •
Nearest metro: Bourse (Line 3), Louvre (Line 1) • Tel: 01 42 97 48 75 • Major
credit cards • Morning snacks, lunch and à la carte teas • E

Wherever you choose to be seated, you will be looked after by Robert Middleton, Scots Master of Ceremonies. Your tea will be served English style, with the leaves in the teapot, and your three-tier cake stand will be decked with all the usual afternoon luxuries. On the lower layer you'll find savories including mini brioches filled with chicken and tomato or egg mayonnaise, double-decker cucumber sandwiches, and smoked salmon. The middle layer holds a display of little biscuits, cakes, and chocolate delicacies, and on the top are arranged pots of jam and cream ready to spoon onto plain and fruited scones. For a special occasion, add a glass of Ritz pink champagne.

Teas offered are Earl Grey, Lapsang Souchong, Huengpin Jasmine, Sencha, Darjeeling, and Bourbon Rooibos.

• Tea lounge and bar in five-star hotel; tea served every day 3-7pm • Reservations essential • Guests must be suitably dressed. • Nearest metro Concorde (Lines 1, 8, 12), Tuileries (Line 1) • Tel: 01 43 16 33 63 • Major credit cards • www.ritzparis.com • Tea by the pot, tea à la carte, afternoon tea • EEE

Cador
Arrondissement: 1e
2 rue de l'Amiral-de-Coligny, Paris 75001

Set in the street behind the imposing walls of the Louvre and close to the Seine, Cador is a treasure of a tea room. It is set in a mini-version of what could be one of the classically beautiful rooms you may see inside Versailles or the Louvre Palace. The

small room appears much larger due to the tall gilded mirrors that line the walls, and the classic, very Parisian tables provide plenty of space on which to arrange a selection of amazing pastries and cakes. Proprietress Sophie Cador is herself perfect for the role of queen or empress, ruling over this small domain that was featured regularly in episodes of the detective series, *Maigret*, on television in the 1970s. She is full of fun and chatter, exchanging banter with her customers and bustling in and out of the kitchen bringing pots of tea and delicious things to eat. The teas are wrapped in muslin and brewed in white porcelain pots. Teas include Ceylon, Darjeeling, Earl Grey, and Lapsang Souchong.

• Classic tea room and pâtisserie retail counter open Tues.-Sun., 8:30am-7:30pm • Nearest metro: Louvre (Lines 1 & 7) • Tel: 01 45 08 19 18 • Major credit cards • Teas, savory and sweet dishes à la carte • E

Park Hyatt Paris - Vendôme
Arrondissement: 2e
5 rue de la Paix, Paris 75002

Visit the Park Hyatt and you will find yourself in a space that is not just a hotel but also a contemporary art gallery. An eclectic mixture of paintings and sculptures surrounds you while you relax over dinner or enjoy tea in the beautiful, subtly understated style of Les Orchidées restaurant. Everything – plates, glasses, furnishings, lights, carpets – has been specially created by well-known artists and designers to make this a unique space.

Settle into one of the charcoal or amethyst colored armchairs or gold sofas and nibble your way through the Thé Complet Park Hyatt, which offers a selection of little open sandwiches with duck foie gras, prosciutto, smoked salmon and Burgundy truffles, scones and madeleines, and a beautifully presented platter of crème brûlée, fruit jelly, fruit tartlet, red fruit savarin, baby rum baba, macaroons and chocolate velours. Or choose a pot of tea and one of the edible works of art that sit temptingly on the dessert trolley. This is the hard part! Would you prefer the chocolate bauble with lime, caramel, chocolate cream and soft, melt-in-the-mouth violet flavored jelly? Or do you fancy the sugar-cane-hollow filled with rum baba or the 'Not Guilty' (so called because it contains no sugar and no flour) of pineapple and papaya marmalade with panna cotta and green tea jelly? Perhaps you would like to spoon your way into a glass tube filled with 'snowballs' of mandarin jelly covered with white chocolate. These are as inventive and artistic as everything else, and you will find it hard to resist trying at least one.

(Continued on page 25)

Toraya
Arrondissement: 1e
10 rue Saint-Florentin, Paris 75001

When Toraya was opened a little over a quarter of a century ago in a side street just around the corner from the Louvre, the aim was to tempt French connoisseurs to try *wagashi* (traditional Japanese pâtisseries) for the first time. Today, seventy percent of the clientele is French and those early efforts have obviously been rewarded. Before you go inside to try some for yourself, take a moment to admire the window display. It is usually very simple but inspirational and quite, quite beautiful.

Step though the door, leave Paris behind, and find yourself in a delicate, minimalist part of Japan. The colors are dark wood, beige, and orange. The style of the intimate lounge has hints of 1960s retro but with a subtle Japanese artistry that lends a soothing, warm, discrete ambience. Wonderful Japanese teas are served in Japanese pots and brought to the table with lacquer or earthenware bowls neatly arranged on sleek trays. The savory foods are perfect for a light brunch or lunch – noodles, miso soups, steamed vegetables. The low calorie pâtisseries combine favorite Japanese ingredients (chestnuts and adzuki bean paste) to create small sweetmeats that are perfect with Matcha, Sencha or Bancha. Enjoy the little jewel-colored pyramids known as *lumières du Louvre*, little squares of clear paste (Jeux d'Ombres dans les Herbes Aquatiques) with tiny fish that appear to be swimming inside, and Tournesol, the head of a sunflower with a center made from red bean paste and bright yellow petals from a different bean paste. If you need something cool to refresh you, try the ice cream drenched in green matcha tea and strawberry syrup. In winter, warm up with matcha-flavored hot chocolate.

The tea list offers Sencha, Gyokuro, Bancha, Matcha, Genmaicha, Hojicha, Soba-cha, Darjeeling, Earl Grey, Ceylon, Jasmine, and various herbals, juices, coffees, and hot chocolates.

• Tea room open Mon.-Sat. 10:30am-7pm • Nearest metro: Concorde (Line 1, 8, 12), Madeleine (Line 8, 12, 14) • Tel: 01 42 60 13 00 • Major credit cards • www.toraya-group.co.jp/paris • Japanese savory and sweet dishes à la carte • EE

24

The tea list includes Darjeeling Tukvar, Ceylon Coop Lanka, Ceylon Decaffeinated, Assam Mokalbari, Genmaicha, Lung Ching, Yunnan Dian Hong, Taiwanese Lapsang Crocodile, and Christmas blend. There's also Once Upon a Time Christmas blend (black tea with cinnamon, apple, almond, ginger, marigold petals), Pouchkine (citrus flavored blend), and Park Hyatt blend (black and green teas with jasmine, ylang-ylang, citrus and naraquila flavoring). Other selections: It's a Fine Story blend (China and Ceylon teas blended with figs, bergamot, citrus, lotus, pitanga and sunflower petals), Orchidée (China tea with orchids and jasmine flowers), Finest Earl Grey, Dragon Jasmine, and Tea of the Season.

• Tea lounge in five-star hotel; tea served every day 3-7pm • Nearest metro: Opéra (Line 3, 7, 8) • Tel: 01 58 71 12 34 • Reservations recommended • Major credit cards • www.paris.vendome.hyatt. com • Thé Complet Park Hyatt (Tea French style), tea à la carte • EE

Place Numéro Thé
Arrondissement: 1e
20 place Dauphine, Paris 75001

Diane Mordacq le Blanc is the most charming of hostesses. She moves from table to table with her radiant smile and generous disposition, making everyone feel as if they are guests at her special party and making sure that they all have a splendid time. Her treat of a tea room is a tiny jewel set in a poetic triangular-shaped square where elegant private houses are interspersed with boutique restaurants. It's a little corner of Parisian tranquillity. Choose a table on the pavement or in the pretty tea room with its sunny yellow walls and whimsical trompe l'oeil effects, curled metal chairs, and large gilded mirror.

Lunchtime menus vary, but there is usually a selection of salads, quiches, platters of cold meats, traditional tagines or braised meat dishes and fresh vegetables. Desserts and cakes also vary from day to day and include fondant chocolate pudding with crème anglaise, crumbles, meringues, and old-fashioned ice creams. The high quality, loose leaf teas include a Gunpowder and mint blend, Darjeeling organic from Makaibari Estate, Japanese Hojicha, Yunnan Grand Muraille and one or two flavored blends. They are brewed in a large paper filter inside the teapot so that customers can remove the leaves when the tea has reached a suitable strength and flavor.

• Tea room open Mon.-Tues., Thurs.-Fri., sometimes Sat., noon-6pm • Nearest metro: Cité (Line 4), Pont-Neuf (Line 7), Saint Michel (Line 4) • Tel: 01 44 07 28 17 • Major credit cards • www.placenumerothe.com • Lunch, à la carte teas • E

The upper chapel of Louis XIV's Sainte-Chapelle, located within the Palais de Justice complex on the Île de la Cité, is resplendent in its Gothic architecture. Light, color, and space blend to inspire a sense of harmony between art and religious faith. Place Numéro Thé, tucked away on a quiet neighboring street, is the closest tea room to this glorious jewel.

Ventilo Galerie

Arrondissement: 2e
27b rue du Louvre, Paris 75002

Armand Ventilo has created a very pleasing blend of fashion, art, and tea that invites visitors to browse clothing on the ground floor before climbing the sweeping staircase to the first floor art gallery and tea room-restaurant. When he opened in 1986, his philosophy was to create a space that subtly combined beauty, art, gastronomy, interior design, and fashion with a harmony and style appealing to people of all ages and all types.

The gallery holds monthly exhibitions of unusual drawings, paintings, and designs. From the intimate exhibition space, customers pass into the tea room, where they are welcomed with grace and courtesy as if visiting a friend at home. The room is instantly appealing with its curvy chairs in pink and yellow, the eye-catching pale pastel colors of the glasses and platters, and the bright blue, swirling dragon that sweeps across one wall. These touches of brilliance are set against the natural colors of cane chairs, brown wood tables, wooden parquet floor, and exquisite Asian carved wood panels. It's a room that makes you smile.

During the years when France held sway as a colonial empire, the nation developed especially strong ties with Indochina. Those connections remain evident today, as Paris is home to many exceptional tea rooms with direct ties to Japan, China, and other areas to the east.

The varied and colorful tones of the room are echoed in the colors and tastes of the beautifully presented foods and dishes. You'll find elegant portions of tomato gazpacho, tandoori tuna, beef carpaccio with tofu and grilled sesame seeds, and desserts of fresh fruit salads, pecan brownies with rose flavored chantilly cream, and an orange blossom and pomegranate cream.

A dozen or so light loose leaf teas have been carefully selected to reflect the lightness of touch here. There are no robust English Breakfasts, just fine, subtle jasmines, oolongs, greens, and lighter blacks from Darjeeling and the high mountains of Sri Lanka.

Teas include Pai Mu Tan, Lung Ching, Panyong, Puerh, Japanese Sencha, Darjeeling, Ceylon Nuwara Eliya, Oolong Imperial, and Jasmine Imperial.

• Fashion store, art gallery and tea room, open Mon.-Fri. 10:30am-6pm; closed Sat.-Sun. • Nearest metro: Madeleine (Lines 8, 12, 14) • Tel: 01 44 76 82 97 • Major credit cards • Morning snacks, lunch, tea à la carte • EE

Boulangerie or Pâtisserie: saying (and finding) food in France

A refresher course of terms and brews for enjoying tea and accompaniments in the City of Lights.

Blue-green (bleu-vert) teas - The French term for oolong teas.

Boulangerie - General term referring to breads, croissants, brioches, and rolls. Also the place that sells breads (a bakery).

Brasserie - Place of refreshment that is a cross between a bar, a restaurant, and a café.

Brioche - Soft buttery, slightly sweet, dough eaten toasted or warmed at breakfast.

Chocolatier - Person who works with chocolate and creates delicious chocolate confectionery.

Cake - To the French, "cake" is always loaf-shaped, not round or square.

Fromage blanc - A fresh, white, creamy cheese made from whole or skimmed cow's milk; often eaten in France as a light dessert with honey and fruit.

Macaroons - Small, round, melt-in-the-mouth meringue-like macaroons with fondant centers; available in a variety of flavors. A Parisian specialty.

Madeleines - Small sponge cakes in the shape of an elongated shell with small grooves on the top; flavors vary from lemon to orange or chocolate.

Mille feuille - A dessert of multi-layered, fine, flaky pastry (literally, it means a thousand leaves!) with crème pâtisserie or whipped cream between the layers.

Opéra - Very thin layers of almond sponge, coffee buttercream, and coffee mousse, covered with dark chocolate glaze.

Pâtisserie - General term referring to cakes and pastries. Also, the place that sells such goodies. A *pâtissier* is a pastry chef.

Religieuse - Traditional French pastry consisting of two orbs of choux pastry, one slightly smaller and sitting on top of the other, filled with creamy custard and topped with sugary, glossy icing; usually coffee or chocolate flavored.

Salon de thé - A general phrase meaning that tea is available in a café or brasserie. Not a guarantee of quality; many establishments that use this phrase offer only poor teabags.

Tarte - A large, round pastry case. When savory, this is rather like a quiche; when sweet, it's a tart or pie.

Thé Complet - Set tea for a set price.

Thé parfumé - Flavored tea.

Wagashi - Japanese sweetmeats usually made with red bean paste and other bean pastes.

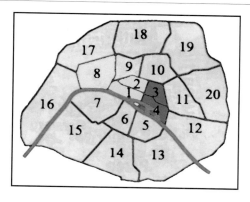

Notre Dame and Île St. Louis

Arrondissements 3, 4

Ancient bridges link the left and right banks to the two charming islands that lie peacefully at the very heart of the city. Stroll from Notre Dame across the river to the chic Marais neighborhood and beyond to discover tea venues that range from the oriental and colonial to the bohemian and endearingly eccentric.

La Charlotte de l'Isle
Arrondissement: 4e
24 rue Saint-Louis-en-l'isle, Paris 75004

This is a place of fantasy and poetry created by Sylvie Langlet, poet and ceramicist. It is an enchanting little tea room just big enough for a dozen people to sit surrounded by objects that seem to have popped out of odd dreams and gathered here to amuse. There are puppets dangling on strings, creatures perched on the edge of shelves, good witches, dolls, and fairies flying on threads from the ceiling, baskets and boxes from India, charming little pictures propped against the wall, and masks from carnival and Halloween. Against the wall stands a piano with music waiting to be played, and the small parlor beyond is crammed with little tables and is full of warmth and friendly

chatter. On Thursdays, the puppets come to life to fascinate and amuse children, whose mothers enjoy the make-believe as much as their offspring.

Sylvie also collects chocolate molds, and there are things made from chocolate everywhere. A chocolate elephant sits in the window, chocolate insects gaze at you from the counter, wands of orange peel dipped generously in chocolate ask to

be eaten, a silver dish is filled with violet and rose petals crystallized and coated with a smooth chocolate layer, and rich chocolate cakes demand a place on the tea table! The small glass counter is always full of succulent fruit tarts, pecan pies, generous lemon tarts, and more chocolate cakes. Customers stand transfixed, and choices are hard to make.

The ladies who look after you here are kind and thoughtful, like favorite aunts or older sisters. If you want a change from tea, choose Sylvie's thick, dark, velvety, hot chocolate. It is so rich that you think you will never be able to drink it all, but soon you find the pot and the cup are empty.

The selection of loose teas includes Darjeeling Jungpana, Assam, Taiwanese Oolong Fancy, Ceylon BOP, Grand Yunnan (excellent with chocolate), Lapsang Souchong, Tarry Souchong, Russian Caravan, Keemun, Earl Grey, Brunch Blend of Darjeeling and Assam, and lots of flavored teas.

• Tea room with small retail counter open Thurs.-Sun. 2-8pm. Closed from last Sun. in June until Sept. 15 • Nearest metro: Sully-Morland (Line 7), Pont-Marie (Line 7) • Tel: 01 43 54 25 83 • Major credit cards • Teas and cakes à la carte • E

The cornerstone for Notre Dame was laid in 1163. It was here that Napoleon crowned himself emperor (1804) and Victor Hugo found inspiration for his famed, but fictional, story of a hunchback devoted to his work of ringing the bells.

Dalloyau Lounge Bastille
Arrondissement: 4e
5 Boulevard Beaumarchais, Paris 75004

As at Dalloyau's other shops, customers are tempted by counters full of goodies on the ground floor before reaching the tea room upstairs. Glass shelves hold yoyo macaroons, exquisite cakes, and chocolates. In the tea room, a fuchsia and deep pink theme sets a slightly bohemian tone that appeals to the young people of the district. They come here for tea during the day and drinks or dinner in the evening. Lighting is discreet during the day and soft candle-glow in the evenings. Songs recorded specially for Dalloyau create a Parisian mood that will appeal to anyone who loves an easy and comfortable yet stylish atmosphere.

Teas are brewed in a knotted paper filter that you pop into the pot and leave for as many minutes as you require. The choice includes Ceylon OP, Darjeeling GFOP, Assam GFOP, Grand Yunnan, Lapsang Souchong, Mint tea, Jasmine, Mélange Dalloyau (blend of China and Indian teas flavored with citrus fruits), and Un Printemps à Paris (Springtime in Paris blend of Tahitian cherry blossoms, lotus, citrus fruits and figs).

• Tea lounge and pâtissiere open every day 11am-midnight • Nearest metro: Bastille • Tel: 01 48 87 89 88 • Major credit cards • www.dalloyau.fr • Teas and food à la carte • EE

Le Loir dans la Théière
Arrondissement: 4e
3 rue des Rosiers, Paris 75004

The bohemian style fits Paris, and this tea room offers another excellent example of how to make customers feel comfortable and part of a family of like-minded acquaintances and friends. The long room is filled with a sort of Granny's-attic mixture of big old armchairs and sofas, dining chairs, and low rectangular or round coffee and dining tables. The walls are absolutely crammed full of posters, old adverts for concerts, shows, and events, and more paintings are hung over all of that. The lights are always low, the sideboards are always laden with huge fruit flans and tarts, and the atmosphere is intellectual and unpretentious, sort of a student common-room crossed with the scruffiness and comfort of a neglected stately home. Some groups of people chat, discuss, and argue. Others read or work as waiters weave their way between tables delivering salads, platefuls of pasta, generous wedges of fig tart or apple strudel, and trays carrying silver teapots and white porcelain cups and saucers. If you want comfort and an easy-going atmosphere, this is the place for you.

Teas include Yunnan, Keemun, Jasmine, Sencha, Oolong, Russian, Lotus flavored black, and Darjeeling.

• Slightly bohemian tea room open every day 11:30am-7pm • Nearest metro: Saint-Paul (Line 1) • Tel: 01 42 72 90 61 • Major credit cards • Lunch, desserts, cakes, and teas à la carte • E

Bohemian? The term as it applies to the arts is a timeless concept that knows no geographic boundaries. In this context, Bohemia is not a place on a map but any community of people whose paramount interest is literary or artistic in nature. Consequently, the lifestyle of the bohemian tends to differ dramatically from what might be considered established norms.

31

Mariage Frères

Arrondissement: 4e
30 rue du Bourg-Tibourg, Paris 75004

One of the oldest and most highly respected tea companies in Paris, Mariage Frères offers the best of world teas in an environment that is intelligent, informative, and classy. The service is impeccable, customers are respected, and one senses an extreme dedication to all things tea. The three shops are similar in style, carrying a vast range of loose and bagged teas, tea jellies, perfumed candles, tea sweets, tea flavored biscuits, books and of course all sorts of teapots. The loose teas are stored in large black and gold canisters that are ranged behind the wooden counter. Staff members, in their white or cream linen suits, are constantly busy weighing out the leaf, answering questions, and advising the steady stream of customers. Don't miss the museum upstairs with its fascinating and nostalgic collection of tea-advertising material, tea packaging, caddies, and brewing equipment.

Here in the Marais, the tea room is on the same floor as the retail counter. As you step from the sombre lighting of the shop to the airy lightness of the tea room, you will find yourself in a colonial setting. There are Indochinese tea posters on the walls, sweeping potted palms, ceiling fans, crisp white linen tablecloths, and Lloyd Loom conservatory-style chairs. Displayed on a central table are scones, little tartlets, small cakes, and fruit flans of all descriptions topped with swirls, circles, and fans of brightly colored fruit, plus extravagances of cream and chocolate. Once you have chosen your tea from the longest tea list anywhere in Paris (probably in the world), the leaf will be lovingly brewed by a trained tea specialist who measures the tea, checks the temperature of the water, times the brew, decants your liquor into a warmed cosi-ware teapot, and delivers it to your table with a small white china cup and saucer. Tea drinking doesn't get better than this!

The tea list includes more than 500 white, green, oolong, black, blended and flavored teas from India, Sri Lanka, China, Taiwan, Nepal, Japan, Korea, Indonesia, Bangladesh, Malaysia, Thailand, Burma, Vietnam, Russia, Turkey, Argentina, Brazil, Cameroon, Kenya, Mozambique, Malawi, Uganda, Rwanda, Tanzania, Zimbabwe, South Africa, Australia, Papua New Guinea, and Mauritius.

• Tea room, extensive retail counter, and small tea museum. Tea room open every day noon-7:30pm; retail counter open every day 10:30am-7:30pm • Nearest metro: Hôtel de Ville (Lines 1, 11) • Tel: 01 42 72 28 11 • Major credit cards • www.mariagefreres.com • Buy tea by the pot or choose purchases from the extensive range of teas from all over the world, exclusive flavored blends, tea accessories, jams and jellies, biscuits, candles, gift boxes • EEE

Pain d'Épice

Arrondissement: 4e
12 rue Jean-du-Bellay Paris 75004

The location for this sunny little shop is at the heart of Paris on Île St. Louis, the smaller of the two islands in the middle of the Seine, tucked behind the one that is home to Notre Dame. When you've strolled through the cathedral gardens and crossed the footbridge that links the two islands, drop into Pain d'Épice for a cup of tea or an ice

cream. The environment is not particularly chic or elegant, but it is friendly, comfortable, and bright, with seats on the pavement – an ideal spot for watching the world wander by.

Tea is brewed with the leaves inside a metal or porcelain pot and comes with a strainer and a chunky blue cup. The lunchtime menu seems to feature snails (although that might just have been the special of the day, which everyone was tucking into when I was there), but there are also lovely fresh salads, omelets, soups, and pasta followed by pancakes, pastries, and scoops of really excellent ice creams in about twenty different flavors. When you're ready, stroll around the corner into a street packed with specialty food shops selling chocolates, wines, cheeses, pâtés, breads, and cakes.

The quite basic list of teas includes Ceylon, Darjeeling, Lapsang Souchong, Earl Grey, Red Fruits, and Mint tea.

• Tea room and restaurant open every day noon-10pm • Nearest metro: Pont-Marie (Line 7) • Tel: 01 43 25 64 63 • Major credit cards • Lunches and teas à la carte • E

Shopping Sites for Tea Lovers

Le Palais des Thés

Arrondissement: 3e
64 rue Vieille-du-Temple, Paris 75003

Le Palais des Thés was set up by a group of tea lovers who wanted to be totally involved in every aspect of their company. They decided they would go to the growing regions themselves to learn about the teas and choose the best for their shop and mail order businesses. They now pass on their knowledge through their shop, website, and a tea school that offers oportunities to taste and understand the manufacture of all the different categories. Staff members are happy to discuss their teas and the lives of people who grow and manufacture them, the climate and countryside, the local situation, and the history of each tea-growing region.

The tea list offers more than 200 different teas from almost every single growing region around the world, including the more obscure such as Bangladesh, Sikkim, and Mauritius. If you like oolongs, there are more than 18 to choose from; if green is your preferred type, Le Palais offers more than 20; and if you prefer classic or contemporary flavored teas, the list includes more than 80.

- Tea retail shop open every day 10am-8pm
- Nearest metro: Hôtel de Ville (Line 1, 11) • Tel: 01 48 87 80 60 • Major credit cards • http://palais-prod.cvf.fr/eng (Excellent website) • Loose leaf teas, tea caddies, teapots, cups and saucers, filters, scoops, gingerbread, jams and jellies, tea gifts.

Art lovers have plenty of options in the Marais area, including the Picasso Museum, the Carnavalet (French art and history), and the Pompidou (modern art).

Terre de Chine
Arrondissement: 4e
49 rue Quincampoix, Paris 75004

Madame Wang Li Juan presides over this elegant and stylish Chinese tea shop that is almost an art gallery of beautiful objects. Everything is displayed with an appreciation of color, texture, and tea's important place in Chinese culture. Wang Li Juan is passionate about her work and clearly enjoys talking to customers about the teas she sells. She knows every detail of the provenance, the exact season when the leaves were harvested, the perfect method of brewing, and stories behind the tea's origin. Unusually, each tin that holds tea is marked with the exact date when the tea was picked. The shop is filled with wonderful Yixing teapots, calligraphy and calligraphers' brushes, tea jars, bowls, platters, dishes, wood carvings, fans, and furniture. It is a place to linger and browse, to learn and appreciate.

Choose from the wide range of white, yellow, green, oolong, black, compressed, and puerh teas. The list includes Huan Shan Mao Feng, Lung Ching, Ti Kuan Yin, Dao Hong Pao, Jin Ya Hong Cha, Yunnan, and Eight Treasure Tea.

- Chinese retail shop open Tues.-Sat. 11am-7pm • Nearest metro: Châtelet (Lines 1, 4, 7, 11) • Tel: 01 42 71 25 71 • www.terredechine.com
- Major credit cards

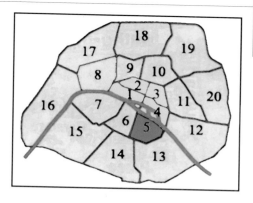

The Latin Quarter

Arrondissement 5

This is the district of books and students, intellect and art, an area of mixed interests and nationalities where Arabic meets European and older academics mingle in tea rooms and brasseries with younger newcomers, philosophizing over glasses of wine and shared pots of tea.

La Fourmi Ailée
Arrondissement: 5e
8 rue du Fouarre, Paris 75005

Set in the heart of the Latin Quarter, La Fourmi Ailée has a gentle, poetic charm that makes lunch or tea a calming, soothing experience. The decor features high ceilings, walls lined with bookshelves that climb up far too high to reach, soft Provencal blues and yellows, and a ceiling the color of a blue sky on a clear summer's day. There's a hint of fantasy and a large iron statue of the Buddha. The background music is French, Latin, or jazz, the service is efficient and very friendly, and the clientele quiet and polite. The menu feels just right, and the excellent loose leaf teas are well brewed in a knotted paper filter that can be lifted out of the Japanese Tetsubin iron teapot once the tea has brewed to perfection.

The teas include green China tea, Lapsang Souchong, Tarry Souchong, Yunnan, Keemun,

Jasmine, Grand Assam, Darjeeling, Ceylon, and Earl Grey. A selection of flavored teas includes mango, blackberry, honey, vanilla, caramel, cinnamon, Old Man Blend (Ceylon and China black teas flavored with hazelnut), and Russian Douchka (flavored with citrus fruits).

- Tea room and restaurant open every day noon-midnight
- Nearest metro: Saint-Michel (Line 4) • Tel: 01 43 29 40 99
- Major credit cards • Lunch, snacks and teas à la carte • EE

La Maison des Trois Thés
Arrondissement: 5e
33 rue Gracieuse, Paris 75005

Tea master Yu Hui Tseng, who is from Taiwan, is the only woman among ten Chinese tea masters alive today. Her family has been involved in growing and selling tea for generations, and tea is her life. She goes to Taiwan for six months of every year to travel from garden to garden, selecting the best of the year's offerings from small artisinal producers. She then brings them directly to the Paris shop to be enjoyed as fresh as possible or, in the case of puerh teas, to be aged in a process she can personally oversee. Her temperature-controlled basement holds more than 1000 teas!

Visitors to her shop are presented with a list of teas currently in stock, which usually includes more than 400 different varieties. The chosen tea or teas are then expertly brewed Gong Fu style and discussed, allowing customers to educate their palates to the very wide range of flavors and aromas. Yu Hui Tseng's assistant, Fabien Maiolino, came to tea from wine and has an extensive knowledge of the amazing variety available. After instruction from the experts, you are left to perform your own Gung Fu ceremony. Some of the teas here are extremely expensive, but it is well worth spending a premium for such quality. Madame Tseng specializes in China oolongs and offers hundreds of different ones. She also stocks many different white, yellow, and puerh teas.

- Tea retail store with tasting area, open Tues.-Sun. 11am-7:30pm. Closed Mon. • Nearest metro: Place Monge (Line 7) • Tel: 01 43 36 93 84
- Tea tasting 1-6:30pm • Gong Fu tea ceremony and tasting • EE

La Mosquée
Arrondissement: 5e
39 rue Geoffroy-Saint-Hilaire, Paris 75005

La Mosquée is an Arabic tea room set in one of the beautifully decorated halls of the vast complex that holds the Paris mosque. The buildings are grouped into a religious section and a commercial section, and the latter houses a restaurant and shop as well as the tea room. Turn to the right after walking up the white steps at the entrance, and you will find yourself in a hall with terracotta and gilded walls, a painted ceiling, and Arabic archways that separate the main room from a raised side aisle. The pillars and floor are marble, and the furnishings are in an Arabic style – large traditional round brass tables, benches, and cane chairs with soft crimson cushions. Gentle Arabic music creates an authentic atmosphere, making this a popular place to relax and sip mint tea.

A friendly waiter dressed in white shirt, black trousers, and a colorful waistcoat offers little glasses of tea from a large brass tray carried to the tables. In one corner of the room, you may find a group of young men sharing tobacco smoked through a *sheesha* (or 'hubbly bubbly'), puffing amicably away while chatting about the day's news. Other customers sit and read, chat with their children, or browse through a newspaper. A tempting range of traditional sweetmeats is available to accompany your mint tea – baklavas (layered pastry filled with pistachios steeped in honey-lemon syrup), Kunafi (pastry stuffed with sweet white cheese, nuts, and syrup), and Mutabak (a pastry turnover filled with cheese and bananas).

The courtyard holds more chairs and tables. Beyond, a crowded shop sells teapots, tagines, bowls, dishes, jewelry, table wares, and clothes.

• Arabic tea room in mosque complex, open every day 9am–midnight. Closed in August • Nearest metro: Censier Daubenton (Line 7) • Tel: 01 43 31 38 20 • Major credit cards • Sole offering is traditional green mint tea served in glasses • E

Shopping Sites for Tea Lovers

La Route du Thé
Arrondissement: 5e
14 rue Lacépède, Paris 75005

With three shops in Paris, La Route du Thé has expanded the number, variety, and location of quality shops in the city selling a good range of teas. This branch is close to the Jardin des Plantes, so consider taking a walk there before visiting. Like the fourth branch in Versailles and the other two in Paris, this location has a richly exotic aura and a strong connection to Asia in the style of the decor and the range of products. Ceramic and iron teapots are displayed around the store, as are scoops, filters, bowls, and cups. There are interesting things that make tea-time

fun – jellies and jams flavored with Darjeeling, Earl Grey and Russian tea, Earl Grey and almond flavored biscuits, Christmas and Dundee cakes, and various sweets. Mingled amongst all the tea things are fabrics, pieces of furniture, and decorative objects. This is an excellent place to come for gifts as well as for teas. Next door, La Route du Soie (The Silk Road) offers decorative objects from Asia.

The tea list in La Route du Thé includes more than 300 from India, Sri Lanka, Nepal, China, Taiwan, Japan, Indonesia, Korea, Laos, Vietnam, Kenya, Cameroon, Tanzania, Burundi, South Africa, Brazil, Argentina, and Mauritius.

• Tea retail store open Tues.-Sun., 11am-7pm. Closed Mon. • Nearest metro: Place Monge (Line 7) • Tel: 01 43 36 63 00 • Major credit cards • www.larouteduthe.com • Retail shop selling teas, tea gifts, teapots, cakes, biscuits, jams and jellies

La Route du Thé
Neighborhood 5e
5 rue de la Montagne Saint Geneviève, Paris 75005

A little closer to the center of Paris than the other two branches of La Route du Thé, this shop is ideally placed to sell tea to the hundreds of students that mill around the Sorbonne area. It is a fascinating area of the city, and a visit to this branch of the company is a good excuse to wander further. The range of products in the shop is very attractive and includes not just tea but gingerbreads and biscuits, unusual jellies and jams made of figs with China tea, apricots with Sencha, rhubarb and vanilla tea, and pears with Earl Grey. The tea list features more than 100 types from around the world, with more interesting varieties than are often available. There are oolongs perfumed with pistachio or seaweed or a mix of ginseng, cinnamon, cardamom and citrus fruits; greens scented with lotus or with mango, fig and rose petals; black teas blended subtly with red fruits or more surprisingly with rhubarb, lavender, cornflower petals, and red berries. There is really something for everyone here.

• Tea retail store open Mon.-Sat., 11am-7pm. Closed Sun. • Nearest metro: Cardinal Lemoine (Line 10), Maubert Mutualité (Line 10) • Tel: 01 43 25 84 18 • Major credit cards • www.routeduthe.com • Loose leaf teas and teabags, teapots, cups and saucers, bowls, filters, timers, jams and jellies, cakes and biscuits

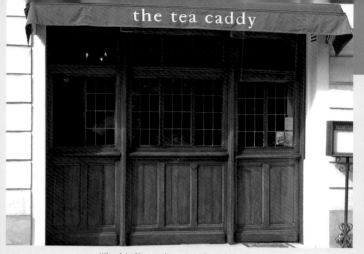

"Sophie Fort, who started working here as a
member of the staff and now owns the business,
has a genius for creating exactly the right
atmosphere with subtle hints of nostalgia.."

The Tea Caddy
Arrondissement: 5e
14 rue Saint-Julien-le-Pauvre, Paris 75005

Taking tea at the Tea Caddy is very much like sitting inside an old-fashioned English caddy. Once inside this old enchanting room, you leave Paris behind and become very English. The tea is served in traditional blue and white willow pattern teacups and saucers just like your grandmother always used. Everything is immaculate and of true English style, from the yellow linen table cloths and Tudor wooden panels to the small copper chandeliers and the pretty orange lampshades that cast a lovely glow over the tea room.

Sophie Fort, who started working here as a member of the staff and now owns the business, has a genius for creating exactly the right atmosphere with subtle hints of nostalgia. The history of the shop, which goes back to 1928, speaks for itself in the charming leaded windows, the old fireplace and mantelpiece, the pictures, and the elderly customers who have been chatting over tea here for 50 years or more and who have fascinating tales to tell. Locals say that the cellars connect up to other buildings in this corner of town and that, during the war, the English and French resistance could run from one house to the next to escape from the Germans.

If you lunch here, choose an omelet or salad with salmon or goat cheese, a vegetable gratin, or a Tea Caddy sandwich. In the afternoon, enjoy a very English tea of really good scones with clotted cream and a choice of jams (rhubarb, strawberries, cherries, or raspberries), or toasted buns and muffins with butter and cinnamon.

The teas are excellent and are brewed in an infuser inside the pot so that customers can take control of the strength and flavor of the infusion. The list includes Darjeeling Spring Flush GFOP1, Ceylon FOP, Yunnan Celeste TGFOP, Keemun, Gyokuro, Yu Xue Ya China white, Dian Hing Gong Fu Yunnan, Xian Xia Lan Cui China green, and Puerh 1994.

• English-style tea room open every day except Tues., noon-7pm. Closed Dec. 24-26 • Nearest metro: Saint-Michel (Line 4) • Tel: 01 43 54 15 56 • Major credit cards • www.the-tea-caddy.com • Lunches, teas à la carte, set English style tea • E

"Vivien Messavant owns this truly wonderful shop
where the retail area is a joy and a feast for the eye!
Beyond the shop is a Chinese tea room that serves
heavenly dim sum, pasta, savory croissants filled
with shrimps, really excellent desserts, and fabulous teas."

Thés de Chine
Arrondissement: 5e
20 boulevard Saint-Germain, Paris 75005

Vivien Messavant was born in Laos, lived in Taiwan, and at the age of 21 came to Paris to study. He stayed and now owns this truly wonderful shop where the retail area is a joy and a feast for the eye! Beyond the shop is a Chinese tea room that serves heavenly dim sum, pasta, savory croissants filled with shrimps, really excellent desserts, and fabulous teas. Vivien designed the shop with such care and attention to detail that you believe yourself to be in Beijing, Taipei, or Hong Kong. The counters and display cabinets in the retail section are filled with enticing Yixing teapots, porcelain bowls, compressed cakes of aged puerh in beautiful boxes, and bright orange tins of loose tea. On the walnut walls of the tea room hang hand-written poems carefully traced out in Chinese calligraphy on pale parchment. The carved wooden tables and chairs are authentic Chinese, and the food and tea are exquisite. Lunch here is heavenly, and shopping for quality tea and equipage is a treat.

The tea list includes twenty-five greens, three whites, three yellows, twenty-five oolongs, five puerhs, fifteen blacks, and forty-two flavored teas. Vivien also sells muslin teabags, jellies flavored with Lapsang Souchong, gift boxes, tea-flavored confectionery, a wide range of teapots, and other brewing and serving table wares.

• Chinese tea room and restaurant with extensive retail area; open Mon.-Sat. 11am-8pm • Nearest metro: Maubert Mutalité (Line 10) • Tel: 01 40 46 98 89 • Major credit cards • Wide range of rare and special high quality teas from China; lunch and teas à la carte • E

Display Teas

Also called Art Teas, Treasure Teas and Flower Teas, these hand-crafted teas are made from skillfully-tied dried green leaves that are usually shaped around dried flower blossoms and tied carefully with a fine cotton or silk thread. Many Parisian tea shops, such as Thés de Chine, stock a variety of these fascinating creations.

Some resemble neat balls of silvery-green tea with just a hint of pink blossom peaking through at the top. Others are shaped like acorns or clam shells, chrysalises or little braids.

Hidden inside each are pink or yellow chrysanthemum or plum blossom flowers which are revealed as the tea is steeped in hot water and gradually opens in an artistic display of natural beauty. They often have such names as Five Golden Flowers, Snow Lotus, and Budding Flower.

To enjoy these very special teas at their best, place one ball of tea in a large glass or glass teapot, carefully pour on hot (not boiling) water and watch as the leaves begin to open and gracefully unfold.

As the flowers inside also absorb water, they gently rise from their green tea nest and float up into the water. A vase containing one of these visually stunning teas makes a wonderful centerpiece for tea table that you can also consume as a hot beverage.

43

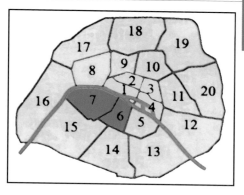

From St. Germain
to Montparnasse

Arrondissements 6, 7

Perhaps one of the most stylish and enticing parts of Paris, St. Germain attracts those browsing for fashionable clothes and accessories, for extravagant works of art and exquisite antiques. Here, too, are some of the most stylish and contemporary salons de thé where inventive chefs work magic with unusual combinations that fascinate and tempt.

L'Artisan de Saveurs
Arrondissement: 6e
72 rue du Cherche-Midi, Paris 7006

The interior of Patrick Loustalot's tea room is sunshine yellow, warm and inviting. It is a welcoming and unpretentious yet sophisticated hideaway where Patrick creates amazing sweet and savory dishes. He manages to combine evocative aromas and flavors to ensure that delicious treats are on the table every time you visit.

This is almost a laboratory of tastes and smells, offering treats for the eye and the palate. Once you have chosen your table and settled into a comfortable, peaceful corner, you will find yourself so beguiled by Patrick's quiet charm that you will not want to move.

Before opening his own tea salon, Patrick was head pastry chef for the Royal Club Evian and

acquired a reputation for his innovative and balanced use of favorite flavors. Since discovering and exploring tea, he has begun to use it as a new ingredient in his menu. He offers customers his signature macaroons flavored with tea and dark chocolate, little biscuits subtly enhanced with puerh, and shots of iced chocolate blended with Japanese Hojicha roasted tea.

Alongside teas from around the world, his list offers some inventively named blends such as B.B. Tea (British Breakfast Tea, which is described as more British than English), Brunch Attitude (a mix of Assam, Yunnan and Darjeeling and an ideal companion to breakfast or lunch), and four teas that reflect qualities of the four elements – Air, Earth, Fire, and Water. Patrick also holds poetry readings and art exhibitions here, and he sells a range of jams, chutneys, honey, sweets, teas, syrups, macaroons, and scones.

The list of more than 40 teas includes Yunnan Shen Xian FTGFOP, Zheijiang Lung Ching, Bi Lo Chun Imperial Jiang Su, Oolong Gopaldhara FOP, Darjeeling Margaret's Hope FTGFOP1 First Flush, Darjeeling Rohini 2nd Flush, Ceylon St. James BOP, Gyokuro Tokujo, Bancha Hojicha, Ying Yang (exotic citrus fruits), Thè et Poèsie (blend of Keemun, Oolong, and Darjeeling), Earl Grey, Jasmine Silver Sickle, Gunpowder Mint, Pai Mu Tan, Lapsang Souchong, and Chung Pouchong.

• Tea room with small retail counter open Mon.-Tues., Thurs.- Sun. noon-6:30pm. Brunch served Sat.-Sun. noon-3pm. Dinner by reservations for 15-30 people • Nearest metro: Sèvres-Babylone (Lines 10, 12), Saint-Placide (Line 4), Vaneau (Line 10) • Tel: 01 42 22 46 64 • Major credit cards • www.lartisandesaveurs.com • Lunch and tea à la carte • EE

The 60-acre Luxembourg garden is one of the most interesting places in Paris to relax and watch people. These palatial grounds, property of the French Senate, are dotted with fountains and statuary. Dalloyau Luxembourg is located next to the garden entrance gate.

Dalloyau Luxembourg

Arrondissement: 6e
2 place Edmond-Rostand, Paris 75006

This branch of Dalloyau is next door to the entrance to the lovely Luxembourg gardens, a perfect place to stroll before or after taking tea. Choose a table by the window in the upstairs tea room to enjoy the view down into the square and across the gardens. Once you have settled in, you won't want to move from your comfortable spot. This location is less sophisticated, perhaps more classic, than the other Dalloyau tea rooms, but it is comfortable and easy with its red, brown, and caramel-colored theme and green and red cushions. In the center of the room is a sculpture of maca-roons in all their usual pastel and acid colors to give the impression of a manicured garden bush in full flower.

Take lunch here and choose from a menu of classic quiches, fish of the day served with steamed vegetables, and traditional French dishes cooked with care and served with style on white and gold platters. Desserts and tea time accompaniments include chocolate mousse, rhubarb tart, vanilla mille feuilles and, of course macaroons.

This branch of Dal-loyau is next door to the entrance to the lovely Luxembourg gardens, a perfect place to stroll before or after taking tea. Choose a table by the window in the upstairs tea room to enjoy the view down into the square and across the gardens.

The tea list is the same as at the other Dalloyau branches and includes Ceylon OP, Darjeeling GFOP, Assam GFOP, Grand Yunnan, Earl Grey, and Lapsang Souchong. You'll find Mint tea, Jasmine, Mélange Dalloyau (blend of China and Indian teas flavored with citrus fruits), and Un Printemps à Paris ('Springtime in Paris' blend of Tahitian cherry blossoms, lotus blossoms, citrus fruits, and figs). Teas are served inside a paper filter, and a little note on the menu warns you not to over brew the teas as they will become bitter if left too long in the pot.

• Tea room and restaurant open every day 9am-7:30pm. Brunch on Sunday • Nearest metro: Odéon (Lines 4, 10), Luxembourg, Cluny La Sorbonne (Line 10), Saint-Michel • Tel: 01 43 29 31 10 • Major credit card • www.dalloyau. fr • Breakfast, morning snacks, lunch and tea à la carte • EE

Delicabar

Arrondissement: 7e
Bon Marché, 26-38 rue de Sèvres, Paris 75007

Delicabar is located on the first floor of the popu-lar Bon Marché department store. It has been of great interest to anyone interested in modern design ever since Claudio Colucci and his partner Hélène Simpson opened the space in 2003. The bright acid green and vibrant flamingo pink, oddly-shaped sofas and wacky metal chairs set a very contemporary, slightly funky character that is reminiscent of an art gallery or museum. In summer, the sense of space and contemporary style extend into the terrace garden, where glass tables are shaded by vast umbrellas and more of the acid green sofas and metal chairs provide plenty of al fresco seating.

Delicabar provides an experience for the senses with its bright colors, unusual shapes, exciting flavors, and fine foods and teas. Tea is used as an ingredient in cakes, desserts, and tartlets, and it is served to refresh and revive those who have shopped for too long. The loose leaf is brewed in a large paper filter that is left inside the pot for the customer to remove when the leaves have steeped long enough.

The tea list includes Lung Ching (Dragon's Well), Ti Kuan Yin, Darjeeling Rohini and Avongrove, Assam Mokalbari TGFOP, Houjicha, Yunnan Imperial, Sencha with red fruits, and mint flavored tea.

• Modern tea salon on 1st floor of Bon Marché department store, open Mon., Wed., Fri. 9:30am-7pm; Thurs. 10am-7pm; Sat. 9:30am-8pm. Closed Sunday • Nearest metro: Sèvres-Babylone (Lines 10, 12) • Tel: 01 42 22 10 12 • Major credit cards • wwwdelicabar.com • Morning snacks, lunch and tea à la carte • E

The Musée d'Orsay (below) houses Europe's largest collection of impressionism paintings. It is located on the Left Bank across the Seine from the Louvre. It is often less crowded and there is an elegant restaurant where you may enjoy a cup of tea and pastries or a light lunch. Avoid the first Sunday of the month when there is no admission fee and the lines are long.

Emporio Armani Café

Arrondissement: 6e
149 boulevard Saint-Germain, Paris 75006

How sensible of Emporio Armani to tempt you with stylish clothes and then guide you upstairs to the Café where you can calculate, while sipping an elegant cup of tea, just how much you shouldn't have spent downstairs. At the top of the silver-walled staircase, a dramatic vase of flowers splashes color against the earthy, neutral tones and clean minimalist lines of the room. The style is sophisticated, chic, and very Parisian. Small square tables are neatly ranged along the walls and are styled with white linen mats and little pots of flowers or plants. Over each table hangs a small cone light on a long flex, shedding a private pool of light on each individual space.

At lunchtime customers can indulge in stylishly simple platters of asparagus, mushroom risotto, wonderfully seasoned pasta, or frogs' legs! For dessert or at teatime, choose the panna cotta with strawberries or the divine little hazelnut meringues, or there's a selection of lovely little pastries. The tea list offers Darjeeling, Gunpowder, Lapsang Souchong, Earl Grey, Japanese Sencha, and Emporio Armani blend (a mixture of lightly smoked black tea with herbs and bergamot). The loose leafed teas are brewed in infusers in the pantry, and the liquor is delivered to the table in beautiful porcelain pots.

• Small tea room on first floor of Armani fashion store, open Mon.-Sat. noon-midnight. Closed in August • Nearest metro: Saint-Germain-des-Prés (Line 4) • Tel: 01 45 48 62 15 • Major credit cards • Lunch, à la carte teas and pastries • EE

Kilali

Arrondissement: 6e
3-5 rue des Quatre-Vents, Paris 75006

The mood of this quiet, calm Japanese tea room is that of a very select, private lounge. Armchairs are low and soft, and the room's colors are muted

(Continued on page 51)

"There are always macaroons at Ladurée, perhaps more the specialty of the house here than at any other Parisian pâtissiere. They come in almost every color, always with a matching cream through the middle."

Ladurée
Arrondissement: 6e
21 rue Bonaparte, Paris 75006

This branch of Ladurée is calmer and more relaxing than the original shop in rue Royale. There is more space and less bustle, so the charm and classic decor has a chance to show itself off, be admired, and speak to you of times gone by. Upstairs is another room decorated in rococo style, a delightful spot to gossip quietly, exchange news, or read a book.

There are always macaroons at Ladurée, perhaps more the specialty of the house here than at any other Parisian pâtisserie. They come in almost every color, always with a matching cream through the middle – pink for the raspberry flavor, yellow for lemon, green for pistachio, white for vanilla, orange for kumquat or mandarin, rich cocoa color for bitter chocolate, a creamy cappuccino color for hazelnut praline, and of course violet for violet with black currant! Munch your way through a plateful here or take a box home for later indulgence.

As at Ladurée rue Royale, the teas are brewed in a filter in the pantry and removed before the silver teapot is brought to the table. The tea selection is interesting if a little hit and miss - Grand Foochow Silver Tip, Lapsang Souchong, Darjeeling Namring, Earl Grey Blue Flower, Mélange Ladurée (black tea with citrus fruits, rose, and vanilla), and Royal Garden Blend (India and China teas with rhubarb, wild strawberries, cornflowers and sunflower petals).

• Tea room and pâtisserie open every day 8:30am-7:30pm • Nearest metro: Saint-Germain-des-Prés (Line 4) • Tel: 01 44 07 64 87 • Major credit cards • www. laduree.fr • Breakfast, morning snacks, lunch and tea à la carte • EE

and easy on the eye. Occasional bright splashes of orange and red appear in the art on the walls, and a hint of aubergine light shines from the lower floor. Small lamps glow softly and are reflected in the gleaming surface of the dark lacquer tables, creating an almost magical glow to the room. An intimate softness is created by the gentle folds of gauze fabric that hang in undulating folds along sections of the wall. The quiet ambience has a touch of Zen about it, allowing time for thought and reflection.

The Japanese menu offers carefully chosen rice dishes, soups, small delicious savory nibbles, and a selection of traditional sweets and green tea ice cream. The excellent teas are brought direct from Kyoto and include four different kinds of Matcha (Senjin, Oguraya, Samidori, Matsukaze), Gyokuro Ichi-Nostubo, Sencha Manryoku, Genmaicha Uzumasa, Kukicha Hashirine, and Hojicha. If you like Japanese style, don't fail to visit.

• Japanese green tea salon, open Tues.-Sat. noon-10pm. Hours on Sun. and public holidays: 1-9pm. Closed Mon. • Nearest metro: Odéon (Lines 4, 10) • Tel: 01 43 25 65 64 • Major credit cards • Green tea and Japanese savory and sweet dishes à la carte • EE

Les Nuits des Thés
Arrondissement: 7e
22 rue de Beaune, Paris 75007

Jacqueline Cédelle's tea room is set inside what was once a baker's shop, and she has created a tranquil resting place with a rather English feel. The double fronted façade has a quiet elegance, and the silver and porcelain teapots in the window give a sign of welcome and invitation that is hard to resist. Pale colors inside set a garden theme that is continued in the linen tablecloths printed with colorful fruits and the carved bunches of grapes that decorate curved chair backs. Corner

Dogs are a regular part of everyday life in Paris, including the restaurant scene. If they belong to a customer, they usually lie quietly under the table or in their owner's lap. If there's an extra chair, no one minds if the dog sits at the table. Everyone admires the pampered creature and he is openly offered a nibble of leftover madeleines. If the dog belongs to the owner of the restaurant, he usually has a casual attitude and ignores most everyone.

51

dressers display the pastel elegance of 1930s cups and saucers, crinoline lady teapots, cake stands and jam pots, and the walls are decorated with pastoral scenes. Visitors pause a while here to be soothed and restored by the calm, pale colors and the sense of rural peace. Of course, it's also the perfect spot to enjoy a pot of tea with a slice of one of the delicious cakes prepared by Jacqueline's daughter, Florence, who does all the baking. An added touch that endears the shop to many people is Luna, Jacqueline's extremely well-behaved sweetheart of a fox terrier who adores being fussed over by customers.

The menu includes generous servings of smoked salmon, chicken, or ham salads, pasta dishes, fruit tarts, crumbles, fruit compotes, scones, and delicious cakes and gâteaux. The tea list offers Keemun, China Gunpowder, Ceylon, Darjeeling, China Rose, Lapsang Souchong, Jasmine, Nuits des Thés House Blend, Blue Garden Blend, Old Man Tea, mint-flavored green, decaffeinated Earl Grey, and other flavored teas.

• Tea room open Mon.-Sat. 11am-7pm, Sun. 3:30-7pm • Nearest metro: Rue du Bac (Line 12) • Tel: 01 47 03 92 07 • Major credit cards • www.lesnuitsdesthes.com • Lunches and à la carte teas; retail loose teas • E

Maison de la Chine
Arrondissement: 6e
76 rue Bonaparte, Paris 7506

More of a cultural center than store—and deco-rated outside with bright red banners to signal its existence—La Maison de la Chine is shop, travel agency, bookstore, cinema, and restaurant. You can browse the retail counter for silk dresses, shirts and scarves, little Chinese slippers, purses, bags, and picture frames before wandering to the restaurant/tea room at the heart of the building. This closeted haven is stunning, with its high ceiling, collage of bright photography on the walls, and amazing sculpted throne-like chairs and carved wooden tables. While you take in the decor and read through the menu, gentle Chinese music calms and soothes. The artistic arrange-ment of beautiful oriental tea wares flirts with the eye and brings a smile-provoking sense of being in just the right place.

The menu is imaginative and the flavors and presentation immense-ly satisfying. You'll find soup with ravioli and crunchy vegetables, bowls of shrimp and prawns with Chinese spices, desserts of praline biscuits with chocolate ganache and chantilly cream, rose maca-roons with raspberries and lychee cream, or a cake made with chestnut preserve and green tea. The tea is brewed in the pantry, separated from the leaves, and then delivered to your table in an earthenware pot with a little bowl that sits on a small lacquered tray. Go for lunch and imagine yourself in China.

The descriptive tea list tempts you with Puerh, Lung Ching Grade 1 & 2, Biluochun Grade 1 & 2, Ti Kuan Yin Grade 1 & 2, Shuixian Water Sprite, Qimen, Yancha, Yin Zhen Jasmine, Gouqi Juhua Lücha, Feng Yan, Le Secret de Buddha (display tea with flowers inside), La Fleur de Jade (display tea with jasmine flowers), Yunnan Dian Hong, Yunnan Lizi Hongcha, Guihua Wulong, and Dersou Ouzala (blend of Lapsang Souchong, star anise and coriander).

• Chinese culture center and store with tea room and restaurant, open Mon.-Sat. 10:30am-7pm • Nearest metro: Saint-Sulpice (Line 4) • Tel: 01 40 51 95 16 • Major credit cards • www.maison-delachine.fr • Lunch, tea by the pot, desserts and cakes à la carte • EE

Mariage Frères Rive Gauche
Arrondissement: 6e
13 rue des Grands-Augustins, Paris 75006

Like the original Mariage Frères location in the Marais, this charming shop houses retail counter, tea room, and tea museum. Decorated in the same style and offering the same range of loose and bagged teas, tea gifts, brewing equipment and books, the store is a treasure trove of both practical and luxury products. Upstairs in the tea room, the gentle glow of the yellow walls, the Chinese carved wood screens, the mix of Indo-chinese tea posters and adverts, and the potted palms create the same colonial theme as in the Marais. The waiters move between the tables in their cool cream linen suits, and the white linen tablecloths are crisp and spotless. The brewing counter sits ready with its bank of tea caddies ranged along the wall and a supply of cosi-ware teapots in their chrome jackets, and customers chat quietly over pots of perfectly brewed tea and delicious pastries.

In the old cellars tucked away in the basement, you will find a Mariage museum of glass cabinets filled with historic packaging, adverts, teapots, caddies, and urns collected from all around the world. It is this link with the past that gives the

Mariage Frères shops their charm. The exceptionally high quality of their products has earned the company respect and affection from international tea aficionados.

The tea list is too long to include everything. There are more than 500 teas from India, Sri Lanka, China, Taiwan, Nepal, Japan, Korea, Indonesia, Bangladesh, Malaysia, Thailand, Burma, Vietnam, Russia, Turkey, Argentina, Brazil, Cameroon, Kenya, Mozambique, Malawi, Uganda, Rwanda, Tanzania, Zimbabwe, South Africa, Australia, Papua New Guinea, and Mauritius. Included are many green, black, oolong, and white flavored teas.

• Tea room and extensive retail counter; tea room open everyday noon-7:30pm; retail counter open every day 10am-7:30pm • Nearest metro: Odéon (Line 4) • Tel: 01 40 51 82 50 • Major credit cards • www.mariagefreres.com • Tea by the pot, extensive range of teas from all over the world, exclusive flavored blends, tea accessories, jams and jellies, biscuits, candles, gift boxes • EEE

Pâtisserie Sadaharu-Aoki
Arrondissement: 6e
35 rue de Vaugirard, Paris 75006

With a minimalist and stylish Japanese décor, Sadaharu is a tiny shop that makes a big impression. The long counter is filled with stunningly beautiful pâtisserie and sweets. There are six white seats where customers can sit at small square tables to drink tea and taste one of those delicacies or decide what to choose to take home. Around the stark interior are ikebana arrangements of twigs, flowers, and foliage to break up the white of the walls, and the glass counter and shelves are laden with little cakes the color of precious jewels. As with all Japanese sweets, red bean paste forms the basis for many of these alluring treats, but exotic fruits, sesame seeds, chocolate, pistachios, coffee, and green tea also play their part in the repertoire.

The teas you can drink here are not Japanese as one might expect but include black teas such as Aoki blend (flavored with apple and caramel), Douce France (cinnamon and orange flavor), Earl Grey, Ceylon, and iced Earl Grey.

• Japanese pâtisserie and tiny tea room selling teas and cakes; open Mon.-Sat. 11am-7pm, Sun. 11am-6pm • Nearest metro: Saint-Sulpice (Line 4) • Tel: 01 45 44 48 90 • Major credit cards • www.sadaharuaoki.com • Japanese *wagashi* (sweetmeats), Japanese teas, pastries, cakes, chocolates, petits fours • E

Rollet-Pradier
Arrondissement: 7e
6 rue de Bourgogne, Paris 75007

Feast your eyes on the fancy foods displayed on both sides of the ground floor deli and pâtisserie (and buy if you wish), and then climb the stairs to the first floor tea salon where intense tones of

"The fragrance of adventure and poetry endlessly pervades each cup of tea."

Henri Mariage (Founder of Mariage Frères)

fuchsia marry with black and cream to create a very tasteful room. Choose a table by the window to enjoy a view of the street while also keeping an eye on the room, where politicians from the nearby Assemblée Nationale, local residents, and other genteel visitors feel at ease in the harmonious and hushed ambience.

Rollet-Pradier is classed among the five or six Parisian pâtisseries famed for their macaroons, so choose from a selection of enticing flavors to accompany your mid-afternoon cup of tea. There are strawberry, raspberry, pistachio, vanilla, lemon, poppy seeds, and chocolate. Tea is brewed in the pantry, and the tea filter is removed before the porcelain pot is delivered to the table. Choose from Darjeeling Organic Tumsong, Darjeeling Avongrove, Ceylon Aislaby, Yunnan Celestial City, Pi Lo Chun Jiang Su, Formosa Dong Ding, Earl Grey Bourbon Palace, and 1859 Blend (Darjeeling and Yunnan) which celebrates the year the company was founded.

• Tea salon located above top-rated delicatessen, open Mon.-Sat. 3-7pm • Nearest metro: Assemblée Nationale (Line 12), Invalides (Lines 8, 13) • Tel: 01 45 51 78 36 • Major credit cards • www.rolletpradier.fr • Teas, pastries and desserts à la carte • E

Tch'a
Arrondissement: 6e
6 rue du Pont-de-Lodi, Paris 75006

The windows of this Chinese-style tea room and retail store are packed full of little Yixing teapots and other Oriental brewing equipage. Before rushing inside, pause and admire, for these tea objects are truly beautiful. Once inside, you will realize that the Chinese theme continues throughout. At the front, the counter holds large red tins of teas that are measured out for home brewing or brewed for consumption in the tea room. At the

Yixing clay is a type of stoneware clay produced in the region near the city of Yixing in Jiangsu province of China. Beginning in the 17th century, Yixing tea ware was commonly exported to Europe. The finished stoneware, tea ware, and other small items are usually red or brown in color. The unglazed pots are ideal for oolong teas.

back, customers sit at carved wooden Chinese tables to chatter over perfectly prepared cups or bowls of tea. The walls are decorated with black and white photos, and all the artifacts and decorative objects are Chinese. The owner, Lui Xian Zhen, was born in Hong Kong, and she has created a little corner of Chinese culture here.

Different categories of tea are prepared by the correct Chinese method in either a covered zhong or a Yixing teapot. The delightful menu gives all sorts of details about these charming, small teapots, how much of each tea to use when brewing, how long each tea should be infused and why, the correct water temperature, and how many infusions may be extracted from the generous leaf. Talk to Lui Xian, and you will find that she knows everything there is to know about these teas, their legends, their manufacture, their history, and the correct method of preparation.

Teas include Mai Mao, Shou Mei, Meng Ding Huang Yan, Jun Shan Yin Zhen, Long Ching, Lû Mei, Liu an Gua Pian, Hong Shan Mao Feng, Dong Ding, Wen Shan Baozhong, Shui Xian, Da Hong Pao, Dong Fang Mei Ren, Keemun, Yunnan, Puerh, Ti Kuan Yin, and many more.

• Tea retail counter and tea room open Tues.-Sun. 11am-7:30pm • Nearest metro: Odéon (Lines 4, 10), Pont-Neuf (Line 7) • Tel: 01 43 29 61 31 • Major credit cards • Rare and special teas from China, teapots and bowls • E

Shopping Sites for Tea Lovers

La Grande Épicerie Du Bon Marché
Arrondissement: 7e
38 rue de Sèvres, Paris 75007

Most of the best tea companies and many categories of tea are represented on the shelves in the food hall of one of Paris' favorite department stores. There are two tea sections. One has shelves of packed tins and cartons from well known companies (Kusmi Tea, Taylors of Harrogate, Tetley, Hampstead Tea & Coffee, Mariage Frères, Les Contes des Thés). In the other section, loose teas from a new company called Quai Sud (South Quay) are weighed for each customer from large tins. The range of choices is excellent, and the service is focused and helpful.

Other small tea outlets and stands are located throughout the store in departments selling table wares and gifts.

• Extensive food hall, open Mon., Wed., Fri. 9:30am-7pm; Thurs. 10am-7pm; Sat. 9:30am-8pm. Closed Sunday. • Nearest metro: Sèvres-Babylone (Lines 10, 12) • Tel: 01 44 39 81 00 • www.lagrandepicerie.fr • Packaged loose and loose teas

Les Contes de Thé
Arrondissement: 6e
60 rue du Cherche-Midi, Paris 75006

Stark white walls are the backdrop for silver tins labeled in acid orange and yellow, with splashes of pink that add even more vibrancy to the color scheme here. In a street that has a number of tea stores and tea rooms, this is the latest to offer a good range of loose teas, jams, honeys, teapots, temperature-controlled kettles, books, and other tea gifts.

Residents are lucky to have such an impressive selection of stores specializing in good loose teas and all the equipment needed to brew and serve them well.

• Tea retail store open Tues.-Sat., 9:30am-7:30pm; closed Sun.-Mon. • Nearest metro: Sèvres-Babylone (Lines 10, 12), Saint-Placide (Line 4), Vaneau (Line 10) • Tel: 01 45 49 45 96 • Major credit cards • Loose teas, teapots, bowls and cups, tea gifts

Kusmi Tea
Arrondissement: 6e
56 rue de Seine, Paris 75006

When Pavel Michalovitch Kousmichoff ("Kusmi") left his village in 1854 to look for work in St. Petersburg, he could not have known that he would find his first job working as a delivery boy for a tea dealer. Despite not being able to read, he learned well and worked hard, and when he married in 1867, his boss rewarded him by offering a small shop as a wedding gift. By 1901, Pavel had opened another nine stores in St. Petersburg and then expanded to London, Kiev, and Moscow.

By 1917, the year of the beginning of the Russian Revolution, he owned 51 shops in major Russian cities. As trouble erupted in his native land, Pavel transferred much of his fortune to Europe and continued to flourish until 1939 when the Second World War disrupted everything. After a long period of ups and downs, the Orebi family has taken what was left of the Kusmi empire and opened this pretty little shop in St. Germain.

With pure white walls and the vibrant colors of the tins, this is an exciting venue selling enticing, brightly-labeled tins of loose teas with a Russian twist, including blends, organic, decaffeinated, smoked teas, flavored teas, blacks, greens, whites and oolongs.

The shop also has a good range of teapots, mugs, cups, teapot stands, caddies and jars, kettles, timers, and scoops. Staffed by lovely, helpful, chatty people, this is a fun tea store selling serious products.

• Tea retail store, open every day 11am-8pm
• Nearest metro: Odéon (Lines 4, 10), Saint-Germain-des-Prés (Lines 4, 10) • Tel: 01 46 34 29 06 • www.kusmitea.com for mail order and information • Major credit cards • Tins and packets of loose teas and tea accessories

Lyne's
Arrondissement: 6e
6 rue Stanislas, Paris 75006

The three sisters who have owned and run this fabulous store since 2004 are absolutely delightful, talented, charming, helpful, kind, welcoming, and very knowledgeable about tea. Parisians in this little quarter had just about given up on ever having their own local tea shop, and now that they have discovered Lyne's, the store is always busy with customers browsing, tasting, chatting, and buying tea.

Originally from China but refugees from Vietnam, the sisters sell a fine range of teas from Japan, China, Taiwan, and India. Some are flown in specially and are available in the shop just a few weeks after the fresh green leaves have been harvested and processed. In one corner of the shop, there is a low Chinese table and stools on which customers can perch to try the different teas before purchasing. Once the tea has been selected, you can spend time wandering around the spacious store to enjoy the vast display of teapots, bowls, cups, dishes, scoops, and caddies from various origins and beautifully set out in glass cabinets. An additional treat is the range of hand-embroidered linens made by Lien Nguyen, one of the sisters.

The three sisters who have owned and run this fabulous store since 2004 are absolutely delightful, talented, charming, helpful, kind, welcoming, and knowledgeable about tea.

Everything here is fine and carefully chosen to add style and pleasure to tea drinking. You will not be able to tear yourself away from the girls' tea empire without spending at least a little money, and you'll want to come back!

The tea list includes Huang Shan Mao Feng (green), Grand Pouchong, Bi Lo Chun (green),

Roi du Tung Ting (oolong), Oolong des Cimes de Li Shan, Meng Ding Huang Ya (yellow), Yin Zhen Bai Hao (white), Lapsang Souchong Imperial, Roi de Puerh, and many more.

• Chinese tea retail store and tasting room, open Mon.-Sat. noon-7pm • Nearest metro: Vavin (Line 4) • Tel: 01 42 22 26 86 • Major credit cards • www.lynes.fr • Wide range of very special, high quality teas and tea wares from China, Taiwan, India, and Japan

Le Palais des Thés
Arrondissement: 6e
61 rue du Cherche-Midi, Paris 75006

Le Palais des Thés shops are always full of people. The bright acid green of the packaging, the amazing array of products, and the wonderful photographs of tea estates on the walls act as a magnet to anyone passing by. It is really hard to resist the desire to find out what the color and display are all about.

The people working in all the shops are passionate about their products, and the entire operation is devoted to passing on information and giving everyone a really good time. Samples of all the teas are ranged along one wall in glass tubes, and the big chunky brightly colored stoppers can be lifted to allow the magic of the different aromas to waft out.

The counters and shelves are full of brilliant gift ideas and useful equipment, so visitors rarely leave empty handed!

The list of teas is extensive and includes well over 200 different types from China, Japan, Taiwan, Indonesia, Vietnam, Malaysia, India, Sri Lanka, Nepal, Sikkim, Bangladesh, Kenya, Rwanda, Zimbabwe, Cameroon, Mauritius, South Africa, Argentina, and Brazil, plus decaffeinated, flavored, puerhs, and compressed teas.

• Retail tea store, open Mon. 10:30am-6pm, Tues.-Sat., 10am-7pm • Nearest metro: Saint Placide (Line 4), Sèvres-Babylone (Lines 10, 12), Rennes (Line 12), Vaneau (Line 10) • Tel: 01 42 22 03 98 • Major credit cards • Loose teas, tea caddies, pots and bowls, measures, filters, cups and saucers, tea gifts • http://palais-prod.cvf. fr/eng (excellent website)

Le Palais des Thés
Arrondissement: 6e
35 rue de l'Abbé-Grégoire, Paris 75006

Though the name is the same as a larger chain that has several sites in Paris, this charming little shop is in-dependently owned. Tucked away on a quiet side street, it has many loyal clients who pop in frequently to top up their tea supply. The window display is eye-catchingly beautiful, and a tinkling chime rings as you push open the door. Owner Julien Speiss and his staff are more than ready to offer advice, answer questions, and brew you something wonderful to try.

The long and very interesting list of between 400 and 500 teas includes some of the very best from notable estates around the world – Makaibari, Castelton, Margaret's Hope, Jungpana, and North Tuckvar in Darjeeling, Aislaby in Sri Lanka, and Huan Shan in China. There also are teas from Taiwan, Bao Zhoing, and Dong Ding – all absolutely top quality. You'll find CDs of music from tea-growing countries, antique samovars and kettles, tea jellies, tea chocolates, gingerbreads, English cakes, tea-fla-vored sweets, infusers, temperature-controlled kettles, caddies, filters, biscuits, and teapots from Japan, China, Taiwan. This delightful haven is full of teas to please the palate and beautiful objects to please the eye.

The list is too long to include everything but the shop sells whites, greens, oolongs, blacks, puerhs, and flavored teas from all the main producing regions of the world.

• Tea retail store open Mon. noon-7pm, Tues.-Fri. 11am-7pm, Sat. 10:30am-7pm • Nearest metro: Sèvres-Babylone (Lines 10, 12), Saint-Placide (Line 4), Vaneau (Line 10) • Tel: 01 45 48 85 81 • Major credit cards • www.tnature.com • Quality loose teas from all over the world, tea accessories, cakes, gingerbread, green tea sweets, jellies and jams. Loyalty card holders get 10% discount.

61

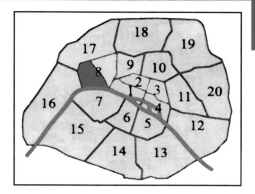

Empire and Republic

Arrondissement 8 (area of l'Arc de Triomphe)

Napoleon lies at rest in the Hôtel des Invalides in the southern corner of this 'quart-
ier'; at l'Arc de Triomphe, Général de Gaulle
is remembered forever in a vast square that
today bears his name. Here you will find all
the finest hotels set on stately avenues
and princely squares that hint at past
elegance and wealth.

Dalloyau Faubourg Saint-Honoré
Arrondissement: 8e
101 rue du Faubourg Saint-Honoré, Paris 75008

Surrounded by fashion shops, classy jewelers, and
antique dealers, this branch of Dalloyau is in one
of the most chic districts of Paris. To get to the
tea room upstairs, customers have to walk past
gorgeous, droolingly-delicious trays of cakes and
chocolates, platters of pâtés, smoked salmon,
roast vegetables, and olives – all prepared for you
to take home and present an impressive meal.

Upstairs, the salon de thé is stylish and very beautiful. The color theme is rich browns, with neutrals
and bright splashes of turquoise in the cushions
and the glasses on the tables. The welcome is
warm, the food excellent, and the quality teas are
brewed in a paper filter in a porcelain pot. Savory
dishes include risotto, smoked salmon or foie gras,
and steamed vegetables. Sweet indulgences have
local names. The Faubourg is a melt-in-the-mouth

concoction of chocolate and vanilla crème brûlée, and the 'Dalloyau' is a dreamy almond meringue with praline cracknel.

Teas include Ceylon OP, Darjeeling GFOP, Assam GFOP, Grand Yunnan, Lapsang Souchong, Mint tea, Jasmine, Mélange Dalloyau (blend of China and Indian teas flavored with citrus fruits), and Un Printemps à Paris ('Springtime in Paris' blend of Tahitian cherry blossoms, lotus, citrus fruits and figs).

• Tea room and restaurant on 1st floor of Dalloyau's pâtisserie and delicatessen; open Mon.-Fri. 8:30am-7:30pm, Sat.-Sun. 9am-7:30pm • Nearest metro: Saint-Philippe-du-Roule (Line 9) • Tel: 01 42 99 90 00 • Major credit cards • www.dalloyau.fr • Breakfast, lunch and tea à la carte • EE

Galerie des Gobelins – Hôtel Plaza Athénée
Arrondissement: 8e
25 avenue Montaigne, Paris 75008

If you are interested in pâtisserie and the creative spirit of the pastry chef, this is an essential place to visit. The glass display cases in the entrance to the Galerie des Gobelins often contain amazing sculptures in chocolate, spun sugar, and other sweet elements essential to the genius of the pâtisserie. When the cake trolley is wheeled to your table for you to make a selection, your eyes will pop! Little winter puddings of pineapple, bananas, and mango with mascarpone cream and jellied fruits, small brioches *tropeziennes*

The streets along the Champs-Elysees are rich in architectural jewels crafted during the decades leading up to World War II.

with butter cream, and crème pâtissière are on display. Also crème fouettée and grand marnier, *driades* (recently voted *champion du monde*) of a whipped praline cream with mandarin, chocolate and marmalade, and macaroons, choux pastry religieuses, and gingerbreads decorated with star anise. The choices invented by the team of 25 bakers and pastry chefs seem endless!

If you can tear your attention away from the pastries, take time to admire the chandeliers, gilded mirrors, pillars, and pink upholstery and drapes. The Galerie is actually named after the impressive 17th century tapestry that hangs at one end of the room. The atmosphere is grand but discreet, opulent but tasteful. The service is charming and quietly thoughtful.

The tea menu includes Ceylon Gunawardena, Grand Szechwan, Grand Yunnan, Grand Formosa Oolong, Darjeeling (Margaret's Hope, Singbulli), Assam, Lapsang Souchong, Pouchkine, Mélange Plaza (Plaza blend with figs, hazelnuts, quince, and raisins), Orangine (green tea with orange and flower petals), Mandarin Jasmine, and Finest Earl Grey.

• Tea lounge inside Hôtel Plaza Athénée where tea is served every day 3pm-7pm • Nearest metro: Alma Marceau (Line 9) • Tel: 01 53 67 66 65 • www.plaza-athenee-paris.com• Afternoon tea, tea à la carte • EEE

Two underground pedways lead to the base of l'Arc de Triomphe where tourists may ascend, for a fee, the 284 steps leading to one of the most spectacular views of Paris. Twelve boulevards of continuous automobiles converge into a mesmerizing labyrinth below.

Hôtel Le Bristol
Arrondissement: 8e
112 rue Faubourg Saint-Honoré, Paris 75008

Any tea lover who visits Paris should not miss Hôtel Le Bristol. The extreme elegance is perfectly suited to an exquisite afternoon tea in an atmosphere of pure aristocratic Parisian chic. This hotel has a sparkling history as the private residence of various counts and countesses who lived here in the years from 1758 to 1925, when it was transformed into a luxury hotel for wealthy travelers. That history causes a shiver of excited pleasure as one strolls through the marbled foyer on the way to the tea room/bar. In keeping with its aristocratic past, and unlike so many hotels that decorate walls with reproductions of famous paintings and fill niches with plaster copies of Greek and Roman sculptures, Le Bristol displays only the real thing. In corridors, lounges, bedrooms, and suites, every piece of art is an original. (Don't miss the stunning portrait of Marie-Antoinette in the tea room.)

This was, for a number of years, the home of the French Tea Club (Le Club des Buveurs de Thé) and, although the club no longer exists, the hotel is still recognized by tea drinkers and press alike as one of the finest tea venues in the heart of Paris. The Bristol Afternoon Tea serves you finger sandwiches, warm scones with butter and preserves, and a beautiful selection of petits fours. The Saturday Fashion Tea (by reservation only) adds to the glamour and shows off the latest collections of prominent designers. Models glide and pose amongst the tables as guests are served tea and pastries specially designed to echo and complement the colors and styles of clothing.

Gilles Brochard, founder of the Tea Club and France's top tea expert, devised the tea list and regularly spends time training the staff to serve tea so as to offer a perfect infusion to all guests. Choose from a carefully balanced menu that offers Darjeeling Singbulli, Assam Dhoomni, Ceylon OP Kenilworth, Japanese Sencha Yamato, Grand Oolong Fancy Dragon d'or, China Keemun, Yunnan Imperial, Jasmine Perle des Mandarins, Grand Foochow smoked Silver Tip, Oolong Ti Kuan Yin, Earl Grey, Russian Baikal, Le Bristol (blend of teas from Sri Lanka, India and China), and Club des Buveurs de Thé (blend of Ti Kuan Yin and Fancy Formosa).

• Tea lounge and bar in Hôtel Le Bristol where tea is served every day 4-6:30pm • Nearest metro: Champs-Elysée-Clemenceau (Lines 1,13), or Miromesnil (Lines 9, 13) • Tel: 01 53 43 43 42 • Reservations recommended • Major Credit Cards • www.lebristolparis.com • Bristol Afternoon Tea, teas à la carte • EEE

Hôtel Daniel
Arrondissement: 8e
8 rue Frédéric Bastiat, Paris 75008

Tucked down a quiet side road not far from the Champs Elysées, Hôtel Daniel has all the peace and charm of a private country residence. Once inside, it is easy to forget the hustle and bustle of the noisy shopping streets just a few minutes' walk away.

The influence here is chinoiserie, and the lounge where tea is served is inviting. There are colorful and luxurious Chinese silk cushions, wallpaper decorated with Chinese birds and flowers, oriental plates and dishes displayed on the walls, carved Chinese wooden furniture, paintings showing Chinese domestic scenes, and fresh orchids.

Settle into one of the cushion-strewn sofas or armchairs, and order your tea and a little savory from the menu of the day. You also may choose from a selection of sweet indulgences such as

(Continued on page 68)

La Galerie, Hôtel George V
Arrondissement: 8e
31 avenue George V, Paris 75008

The opulence and grandeur that awaits you at the Hôtel George V is almost beyond belief. This is one of the most stylish and elegant hotels in the world, and you will feel yourself at the extreme heart of indulgent luxury. La Galerie is to the right of the splendid lobby, and here you are seated in a magnificent armchair and left to choose your afternoon treat.

The George V High Tea (in truth, this is an Afternoon Tea) includes finger sandwiches, a selection of pastries, and excellent scones that are feather light, warm, and served with crème fraîche and strawberry or apricot jam or honey. The High Tea *a la française* offers you a glass of champagne, an assortment of fine savories, little pastries, and a French shortbread biscuit. Or you may take tea à la carte and choose canapés with foie gras, smoked salmon or goat cheese; blinis with sevruga caviar; or finger sandwiches filled with chicken, cheese, ham, cucumber, and smoked salmon.

The impressive pastry trolley is dominated by a chocolate model of the Eiffel Tower. Around its base nestle little tartlets of passion fruit and strawberries, blueberries, and red currants set on a layer of crème pâtissière, tiny white chocolate circles inscribed 'Four Seasons' (as this is a Four Seasons hotel) in dark chocolate, yoyo macaroons, biscuits, madeleines, and various creations in choux pastry. It may take rather a long time to make your choice!

The hotel has thoughtfully considered the requirements of the discerning diner and offers a selection of very rare China teas for those who prefer tea to coffee as an after-dinner *digestif*. Ask the waiter for the tea menu, which gives a wonderful description and tasting notes. Your waiter will brew you one of the puerh, oolong, or jasmine teas that sit on an ornate trolley at the entrance to the restaurant. Your choice of leaf will be brewed with water at the correct temperature drawn from a silver samovar, the brew will be carefully timed, and the perfect liquor will be delivered to your table in a fine porcelain or Yixing teapot.

The tea lists for La Galerie and the restaurant offer Ceylon Kenilworth OP, Assam Gelakey, Darjeeling Bloomfield, Lapsang Souchong, Grand Szechwan, Formosa Grand Oolong, Sencha, Gunpowder, Puerh Liu Bao Cha, Puerh Fu Zi Zhuan, Puerh Millesime, Dian Hing Gong Fu Yunnan, Zheng Shan Xiao Zhong smoked, Zhen Wang jasmine, Oolong Academic Beauty, Oolong Si Ji Chin, Oolong, Mi Lan Xiang, Darjeeling Makaibari, Four Red Fruit flavored tea, Autumn Blend, Four Seasons Blend, Earl Grey, Pouchkine (a mixture of China and Indian teas), Jasmine Ching Hao, and various herbal infusions.

• Tea lounge in exquisite five-star hotel. Afternoon tea served every day 3-6pm
• Nearest metro: Champs Elysées Clemenceau (Lines 1, 13) • Tel: 33 (0) 1 49 52 70 00 • Reservations essential • Major credit cards • www.fourseasons.com • Teas à la carte or set 'High Tea' (a French style afternoon tea) • EEE

Tucked down a quiet side road not far from the Champs Elysées, Hôtel Daniel has all the peace and charm of a private country residence.

melt-in-the-mouth macaroons or dainty little pastries, fresh fruit salad, a platter of red fruits, or a slice of English cake. The quality muslin teabags are brewed in silver art deco teapots accompanied by matching jugs of hot water. Cups, saucers, and plates are of elegant white porcelain with subdued silver-gray stripes. This beautiful room is reminiscent of the days of empire and the Orient Express, perfect manners, and elegant living. Step off the fast-paced main streets and back in time to afternoon tea of days gone by.

Teas offered include Ceylon OP, Darjeeling, Earl Grey, Earl Grey Blue Flower, Fuji-Yuma, Mandarin Jasmine, White Jasmine, Oolong Oriental, Ruschka (Russian style blend with 7 citrus fruits), Buddha Bleu (green tea with cornflower blossoms), Marco Polo (green tea with Chinese fruits and flowers), Casablanca (green tea with Bergamot), Emperor Shen Nung, Opéra, and various herbal infusions.

• Tea lounge in boutique hotel, open every day; lunch and tea served from 3pm • Nearest metro: Saint-Philippe-du-Roule (Line 9, 13) • Tel: 01 42 56 17 00 • Major credit cards • www.hoteldanielparis.com • Tea à la carte • EE

Mariage Frères Étoile
Arrondissement: 8e
260 faubourg Saint-Honoré, Paris 75008

This is the most recently opened of Mariage Frères' three Paris shops and it offers all the same teas, tea gifts, teapots, and tea-flavored biscuits and jellies as the other locations. Everything in the Marais and St. Germain shops is charmingly replicated here – the richly stocked retail counters and the bank of black and gold caddies closely guarding more than 500 plus different teas. Visit the third of the Mariage museums and enjoy the collection of historic tea wares, adverts, and packaging equipment.

When you have browsed your fill, head to the tea room downstairs and choose a slice of one of the delicious flans or tarts displayed irresistibly on the table facing you as you enter. Settle into one of the dark, slatted wood chairs amongst the palms and colonial tea posters and choose one of the many teas. As in the other Mariage tea rooms, the leaf is brewed by a specially trained tea master who skillfully measures out the tea, brews in water at exactly the correct temperature, times the brewing process, and then decants the perfect liquor into a warmed teapot before it is brought to your table. This painstaking method of brewing ensures that every pot of tea is perfect.

The tea list features more than 500 white, green, black, oolong, puerh, compressed, and flavored teas from India, Sri Lanka, China, Taiwan, Nepal, Japan, Korea, Indonesia, Bangladesh, Malaysia, Thailand, Burma, Vietnam, Russia, Turkey, Argentina, Brazil, Cameroon, Kenya, Mozambique, Malawi, Uganda, Rwanda, Tanzania, Zimbabwe, South Africa, Australia, and Mauritius.

• Tea salon and extensive retail counter open every day 9am-7pm • Nearest metro: Ternes (Line 2) • Tel: 01 46 22 18 54 • Major credit cards • www.mariagefreres.com • Tea by the pot, extensive range of teas from all over the world, exclusive flavored blends, tea accessories, jams and jellies, biscuits, candles, gift boxes • EEE

Radisson SAS Hôtel Champs-Élysées
Arrondissement: 8e
78b avenue Marceau, Paris 75008

This classy little hotel hides behind two small clipped trees that stand in tubs outside the discreet main entrance. The color scheme inside is muted, earthy, quietly elegant, and understated. There is no tea lounge, but the excellent restaurant has devised a menu that recommends the most suitable tea to drink with each main course and each dessert. With the veal, choose a rich Yunnan from southwestern China, with the fish of the day try an excellent Ti Kuan Yin, and have a Grand Yunnan with the rich chocolate *Guanaja*. The hotel works very closely with Le Palais des Thés to select teas that suit the dishes and snacks served in the restaurant. It's a refreshing approach, and the teas are well brewed and presented.

The carefully planned list of teas includes tasting notes and background information for Imperial Puerh, Bancha Hojicha, Imperial Grand Yunnan, Imperial Ti Kuan Yin, Grand Jasmine Mao Feng, Superior Japanese Sencha, Sencha Ariake, Assam Maijian, Butterfly of Taiwan, and Darjeeling (Margaret's Hope 2nd Flush).

• Hotel restaurant with annotated tea menu; open all day Mon.-Fri. • Nearest metro: Charles de Gaulle-Étoile (Line 1, 2, 6) • Tel: 01 53 23 43 63 • Major credit cards • www.radissonsas.com • Lunch and dinner, teas by the pot • EEE

A walk down the Champs Elysées brings you to Place de la Concorde and its 3300 year-old red granite obelisk of Luxor, carted here from Egypt in the 1830s. It was on this spot that Louis XVI, Marie Antoinette and thousands of others met their deaths on the guillotine during the Revolution.

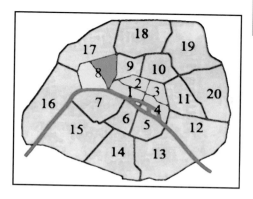

Madeleine

Arrondissement 8 (north of Place de la Concorde)

The Madeleine church stands like a Greek temple in the center of this vast square at the gastronomic heart of Paris. On all sides of the square are fashionable food halls and restaurants, and in the streets that radiate from this focal point are more hidden pleasures just waiting to be discovered.

Chajin—La Maison du Thé Vert Japonais
Arrondissement: 8e
24 rue Pasquier, Paris 75008

American Carol Negiar married Frenchman Xavier and settled in Paris. With their mutual passion for Japanese culture and tea, the pair founded this darling little Japanese tea room in a quiet side street just around the corner from Place de la Madeleine. With careful planning and a touch of magic, they have managed to fit in a counter, tables at which to sit and enjoy traditional Japanese teas and foods, and a miniature version of a Japanese tea house complete with silky tatami matting on the floor and the minimalist elements of the Japanese green tea ceremony. Groups can book to come and celebrate this unique ritual with Carol and her Japanese assistants, or you can just pop in for a bowl of green tea, a green tea ice cream, or lunchtime noodles.

Carol is a vital force behind tea activities in Paris and is keen for people to understand more about Japanese tea, the social importance of tea in Japan, and the joys of drinking and eating green tea. A visit to her shop is an excellent place to start exploring the subject. She offers information, instruction, and a selection of high quality teas, brewing equipment, and tea confectionery.

The teas on sale at Chajin are all Japanese and include Gyokuro, Matcha, Bancha. Hojicha, Genmaicha, Kukicha, Sencha, Fukamushicha, and Ujikabusecha.

• Japanese tea room and retail shop open Mon.-Fri. noon-6pm, Sat. 1-7pm. Closed in August
• Nearest metro: Madeleine (Lines 8, 12, 14)
• Tel: 01 53 30 05 24 • Major credit cards •
www.chajin-online.com • Japanese green and roasted teas, teapots, bowls, brewing equipment, confectionery. • E

Ladurée
Arrondissement: 8e
16 rue Royale, Paris 75008

In 1862, Louis Ernest Ladurée opened a bakery at this address. After a fire in 1871, the shop was restyled as a pastry shop with the interior designed and painted by the famous painter, Jules Cheret. He decorated the ceiling with cherubs and celestial scenes, creating a room so refined and elegant that it attracted all the chic, wealthy ladies of Paris. Today, it still draws a constant stream of visitors. The classic room, with its gilded mirrors, painted panels and heavenly ceiling, is always busy, rather noisy and not particularly relaxing. Upstairs is a calmer room better suited to those customers who wish for a quieter cup of tea.

Loose leaf teas are brewed in the kitchen and removed from the silver pot that is then delivered to the table. With your tea, choose from a savory selection of sandwiches, pasta dishes, smoked salmon, various meat dishes, or to satisfy a craving for something sweet, there are macaroons, mille feuilles slices, ice creams, traditional pâtisseries, croissants, and brioches.

The list of teas includes (in somewhat eccentric order) Yunnan Imperial, Sencha Yamato, Pai Mu Tan, Melange Ladurée (citrus fruits, rose, vanilla, cinnamon), Jasmine, Earl Grey with sunflower petals, vanilla flavored Darjeeling and Assam blend, Namring Darjeeling, Royal Blue Garden (a mix of China and Indian teas with rhubarb and wild strawberries), Royal Fruit tea with black China and Ceylon teas blended with cornflower petals, wild berries, and floral aromas.

(Continued on page 75)

"This 18th century hotel is a living piece of history that transports
you back to the early years of the 18th century, before the French
Revolution ....Take lunch, dinner, or tea here and enjoy superb China
teas, cocktails and excellent wines, and a menu that offers French,
Japanese, and Chinese dishes. "

1728
Arrondissement: 8e
8 rue d'Anjou, Paris 75008

This 18th century hotel has been restored and is more than just a place to go
for tea. It is a living piece of history that transports you back to the early years
of the 18th century, before the French Revolution forced the building's residents
to flee. Built in 1728 by one of Louis XV's chief architects, the house is a perfect
example of a private Parisian *hotel*. The perfectly proportioned salons, leading
one into the other, have wonderfully harmonious dimensions, high ceilings, and
generous windows onto the courtyard. One can easily imagine the most famous
former resident, Madame de la Pompadour, sweeping from room to room to
welcome her aristocratic guests.

The house was in a state of dereliction in 2000 when Lining Yang and her husband
bought it. Restored with great love and attention to detail, it is today a restaurant and tea salon. Each room is decorated with antique paintings, chandeliers,
tapestries, mirrors, candlesticks, sconces, furniture, and sculpture collected from
around the world to marry with the style and architecture of the period.

Guests in the lounge areas are seated in divine red plush armchairs and sofas, and
tea is brought in white porcelain teapots, brewed at exactly the right temperature
for precisely the correct number of minutes and poured into fine white china
cups. Take lunch, dinner, or tea here and enjoy superb China teas, cocktails and
excellent wines, and a menu that offers French, Japanese, and Chinese dishes.
You'll find tuna tartare, sashimi, Coquilles Saint-Jacques, Crab Royale, lobster,
and filet of beef, followed by a choice of excellent cheeses and Japanese style
desserts that include Matcha ice cream, chestnut and red bean jelly and Matcha
gâteau. The tea list includes Imperial Lung Ching, Liou An Gua Pian, Yin Zhen
Bai Hao, Anxi Ti Kuan Yin, Rose Pearls, Jasmine Pearls, Keemun Celeste, Yunnan
Imperial, Ginseng Oolong, and Puerh.

• Restaurant and tea salon open Mon.-Fri. noon-midnight, Sat. 2:30-midnight.
Closed Aug. 15-30 • Nearest metro: Madeleine (Lines 8, 12, 14) • Tel: 01 40 17
04 77 • Reservations recommended • Major credit cards •www.restaurant-1728.
com • Lunch, dinner and tea à la carte • EEE

Hôtel de Crillon, The Winter Garden
Arrondissement: 8e
10 Place de La Concorde, Paris 75008

The Hôtel de Crillon is a jewel of a hotel at the corner of the square that looks across the majestic Place de la Concorde to the river. It stands poised like a quiet observer as traffic and tourists throng the streets and weave their way around the gracious statues and fountains that decorate this vast open space. Afternoon tea is served in a truly beautiful period room that could easily be the setting for Les Liaisons Dangereux or the life of Marie Antoinette. Indeed, it is said that Antoinette came to this sumptuous building for her music lessons. In this setting, it is easy to imagine the duchesses and dukes, counts and countesses, kings and queens who may have perched on the plush red velvet armchairs and sofas, whispering behind their fans, exchanging gossip and scandal, flirting and plotting.

This is one of the most perfect settings for an elaborate, refined afternoon tea served by attentive waiters and waitresses who make sure that you have all that you need. They serve your choice from the à la carte menu that includes little luxury canapés and finger sandwiches featuring Norwegian smoked salmon, duck liver pâté, or caviar or thinly sliced cucumber with cream cheese and cress. The amazing creations on the pâtisserie trolley are sure to tempt. If the set tea is more to your taste, indulge in sandwiches, scones, and madeleines served with butter, honey and preserves. Add a glass of champagne and perhaps your afternoon will be perfect.

An excellent list of teas gives detailed information about the provenance and character of each tea. The offerings include Earl Grey, Darjeeling Jungpana, Ceylon Kenilworth, Jasmine Chung Hao, a lightly smoked tea from China, Assam Mokalbari, Japanese Kokeicha, Formosa Oolong, Grand Sichuan, and Duc de Crillon (a blend of black teas flavored with bergamot, lavender, rose petals, and vanilla). You'll also find Thé des Amours (China tea blended with passion fruit, mango, pineapple, orange and jasmine blossoms), Four Red Fruits (a blend of black teas from China, India and Sri Lanka flavored with strawberries, raspberries, red currants and cherries), Marie Antoinette (a light blend of China black teas flavored with vanilla and caramel), A Gentleman of Deauville (tea blended with orange, bergamot, and chocolate), Marco Polo (a secret blend of black teas with Chinese and Tibetan fruits and flowers), and a few herbal infusions.

• Tea room in a five-star hotel; tea served every day 3:30-6pm • Nearest metro: Concorde (Line 1, 8,12) • Tel: 01 44 71 15 00 • Major credit cards •www.crillon.com • EEE

• Classic tea salon and small retail counter open Mon.-Sat. 8:30am-7pm, Sun. 10am-7pm • Nearest metro: Madeleine (Lines 8, 12, 14) • Tel: 01 42 60 21 79 • Major credit cards • www.laduree. fr • Breakfast, morning snacks, lunch and tea à la carte • EE

La Boulangerie at Fauchon
Arrondissement: 8e
30 place de la Madeleine, Paris 75008

The Fauchon shops are changing their style. Moving away from the recent cerise pinks and stark modern lines, a new concept is being developed to create spaces that lift Fauchon into a realm above the average food hall.

The first area to enjoy the new look is La Boulangerie where all the golden glow, warmth, and wonderful smells of newly-baked bread entice willing customers. Here you can choose breakfast, lunch, or tea from a range of sweet and savory dishes. There are smooth creamy soups, inventive sandwiches, amazing pastries and breads, salads that combine crunchy grains with crisp vegetables, and succulent meats. The range of excellent beverages includes vitamin-rich fruit juices that come in intensely exotic colors, a selection of excellent teas, rich creamy hot chocolates, and various coffees.

Pastry chef Christophe Adam offers favorite French classics such as mille feuilles slices, gâteaux Saint-Honoré and rum babas. His madeleines come flavored with sweet favorites such as chestnuts, chocolate, raspberry and honey and with subtle savory treats including truffles, roquefort cheese, and saffron. His dreamy brioches are unusually flavored with raspberry, lemon, chocolate, or gingerbread. The interior design is startlingly shiny and bright, with triangles of reflective metals creating a kaleidoscope of light and color that

The food halls at Fauchon are an epicurean feast with tea being one of the highlights. The staff is delighted to assist you in sniffing your way through the countless tins of teas imported from across the globe.

enlivens the entire space. It is new, inspired, exciting, and very chic.

Teas served include Darjeeling, Earl Grey, Morning Blend, Fauchon Blend, and a couple of herbal infusions.

• Café–restaurant open Mon.-Sat. 8am-6pm, retail bakery open Mon.-Sat. 8am-8pm • Nearest metro: Madeleine (Lines 8, 12, 14) • Tel: 01 70 39 38 00 • Major credit cards • www.fauchon.com • Breakfast, snacks, lunch, tea à la carte • EE

Minamoto Kitchoan Paris–Madeleine
Arrondissement: 8e
17 place de la Madeleine, Paris 75008

Similar to branches in London and New York, Minamoto Kitchoan Paris is a charming, quiet haven with a shop counter that displays a beautiful range of 50 or so delicate, artistic Japanese sweetmeats known as *wagashi*. The tea room serves delicious Japanese food and pastries in an elegant jewel-box of a room at the back of the shop away from the busy street. The selection of wagashi (all made on the premises by the company's Japanese chef) includes little dome-shaped Sakura Jelly made of cherry flavored transparent jelly inside

The view (below) from Rue Royale gives you a panoramic perspective of the Place de la Concorde and the bridge across the Seine leading to Assemblée Nationale.

which floats a cherry blossom flower. There are tiny cubes of rose flavored Yoshinozakura set with rose petals, green tea, and sesame, and Miwaka-buki filled with white bean paste.

Choose something from the elegant counter to nibble with your tea before you walk past the tiny enclosed garden to the tea room. Or, once settled in one of the neat gold arm-chairs, browse the menu and select a savory soup or rice dish, a salad or sushi, or cher-ry ice cream with cherry jelly or vanilla ice cream topped with a warm Matcha mousse (suitably called Matcha Medi-tation).

If you need help choosing your tea, ask for Marina Sasaki, certified tea sommelier, who will explain the different teas and make sure that whatever you decide to try is brewed perfectly with weigh-ing scales, thermometers and timers, and teapots from northern Japan.

Order a mini version of the Tea Ceremony and you will be served a dainty lacquer tray bearing a bowl of whisked Matcha and two traditional sweets. One is a green bean paste filled with red bean paste; the other is a little snowball enveloping chestnut purée and decorated with a gilded leaf.

The teas offered include Sencha Mori, Genmaicha, Genmaicha-Matcha blend, Kukicha, Karigane-cha, Hojicha, Gyokuro, Matcha, and Iced Matcha.

• Japanese pâtisserie and tea room; retail counter open Mon.-Sat. 11am-7:30pm, tea room open Mon.-Sat. noon -7:30pm (service until 6:45pm) • Nearest metro: Madeleine (Lines 8, 12, 14) • Tel: 01 40 06 91 28 • Major credit cards • www.kitchoan.com • Tea by the pot, mini Japanese Tea Ceremony • E

Ventilo Madeleine

Arrondissement: 8e
13-15 boulevard de la Madeleine, Paris 75001

The décor of this most attractive tea salon artistically combines beautiful carved wooden screens from India with lacquered Chinese chests and iron Tetsubin teapots from Japan. The wooden screens break the space into intimate corners where customers enjoy carefully chosen and finely balanced dishes. Some selections feature prawns, salmon, chicken, tuna, and fresh seasonal vegetables subtly flavored with fresh herbs and spices and served with great finesse. The menu displays the same elegance as at the sister shop (not surprising since both menus were created by the very talented Sylvie Potier), and colors and flavors are creatively devised to amuse both the eye and the palate.

Loose leaf teas are brewed in metal baskets inside silver teapots, and a dish for the basket is provided so the customers may lift out the infuser once the tea has brewed. The choice here includes Pai Mu Tan, Lung Ching, China green Gu Zhang Mao Jian, Yunnan Imperial, Emperor Chen Nung, Sencha, Tamaryokucha, Darjeeling, Assam, Ceylon Nuwara Eliya, Oolong Imperial, Jasmine Imperial, and Esprit de Noel (Christmas blend with sweet winter spices).

• Tea room on first floor of fashion store open Mon.-Fri 10:30am-6pm. Lunch served noon-3pm.

Closed Sat.- Sun. • Nearest metro: Madeleine (Lines 8, 12, 14) • Tel: 01 42 60 20 81 • Major credit cards • Morning snacks, lunch and teas à la carte • EEE

Shopping Sites for Tea Lovers

Betjeman and Barton
Arrondissement: 8e
23 boulevard Malesherbes, Paris 75008

Well established as part of the Paris tea scene, Betjeman and Barton is respected and patronized by large numbers of connoisseur Parisian tea drinkers. The original company was established in 1919 by an Irishman, Arthur Betjeman, and a colleague, Percy Barton, and was taken over in 1978 by Dammann, one of France's major tea wholesalers. The shop has a reassuring, comfortably traditional atmosphere, where customers are treated like old friends who have come to visit.

The dark wooden shelves around the walls are lined with large colored storage tins that contain a range of Ceylons (more than ten), Darjeelings (more than eighteen), Assams (seven), Oolongs (six) and a vast number of teas from China, Taiwan, Kenya, Nepal, Burma, and Japan, plus lots of house blends, flavored teas, tisanes, and herbals. The shop is also packed with gift boxes, teapots, jams, chutneys, chocolates, infusers. scoops, tins, and bowls. It's an excellent place to buy presents and to stock up on your own selection of excellent teas.

• Tea retail store open Mon.-Sat. 10:30am-7:30pm • Nearest metro: Madeleine (Lines 8, 12, 14) • Tel: 01 42 65 86 17 • Major credit cards • www.betjemanandbarton.com • Retail store selling loose and bagged teas and tea related gifts

Betjeman and Barton is respected and patronized by large numbers of connoisseur Parisian tea drinkers.

Hédiard

Arrondissement: 8e
21 Place de Madeleine, Paris 75008

Since 1850, Hédiard has been supplying quality groceries to Parisian gourmets from its location in Place de la Madeleine. The square is, after all, one of the gastrodromes of Paris, with many well known food stores arranged around the vast Madeleine church. Hédiard is often referred to as a 'temple of gastronomy,' and it has the ability to attract you in and not let you go until you have browsed every single inch of the store. Your eyes open wide at the bright scarlet tins that hold the teas; the vast baskets overloaded with packets of coffee, spices, and chocolates; the chrome staircase that leads up to more shelves high above your heads stacked with bottles of wine; and shelf after shelf of jams, preserved fruits, marmalades, cakes, biscuits, foie gras, pâtés, spices, and more.

Hédiard is often referred to as a 'temple of gastronomy,' and it has the ability to attract you in and not let you go until you have browsed every single inch of the store.

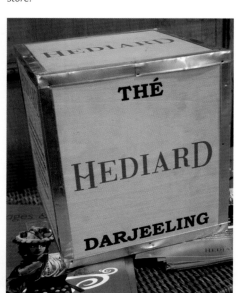

The store sells more than 200 black, smoked, green, oolong, white, and flavored teas as both loose leaf tea and in pyramid crystal teabags. Selections include Ceylon Breakfast, Ceylon Afternoon, Darjeelings, Siliguri Blend Assams, Golden Monkey from Yunnan, Bai Hao Yin Zhen, Jasmines, Moondrops, apple flavored, Four Red Berries, and many more.

• Quality food hall, open Mon.-Sat. 9am-11pm • Nearest metro: Madeleine (Lines 8, 12, 14) • Major credit cards • www.hediard.com • Loose teas and teabags

Les Thés d'Emilie-Twinings

Arrondissement: 8e
76 boulevard Haussman, Paris 75008

When Twinings decided in 1987 that they could no longer maintain their shop in Paris, Isabelle Brandebourger decided to buy it and rename it after her daughter. The shop is not large, but Isabelle has crammed it full of useful and pretty things. She has English teapots, cups and saucers, mugs, French tables wares, Japanese infuser pots, various gingerbreads, spoons, measures, sweets, cards, and tea cozies.

Her range of loose Twinings and other loose teas includes Ceylon, OP, Ceylon BOP, Darjeeling, Assam, Lapsang Souchong, Keemun, Earl Grey,

When Twinings decided in 1987 that they could no longer maintain their shop in Paris, Isabelle Brandebourger decided to buy it and rename it after her daughter.

Gunpowder, Four Red Fruits, Mango, Caramel, Sweet Orange, Vanilla, Russian Blend, Green Mint, and Black Currant.

• Tea retail shop open Tues.-Sat. 10:30am-7pm • Nearest metro: Saint-Augustin (Line 3), Havre-Caumartin (Lines 3, 9) • Tel: 01 43 87 39 84 • Major credit cards • Retail shop selling a good selection of loose and bagged teas from all around the world, flavored teas, teapots, mugs, tea accessories, gifts, gingerbread

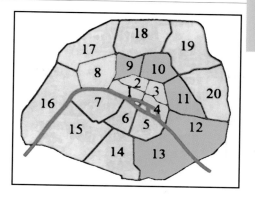

From New Athens to the Bastille

Arrondissements 9, 10, 11, 12, 13

Sweeping around in a crescent that leads through the north and eastern suburbs, discover here the lower slopes of Montmartre, the wide avenues and canals that mark the outer boundaries of the city, and the generous spread of the Botanical Gardens.

La Pharmacie
Arrondissement: 11e
22 rue Jean-Pierre-Timbaud, Paris 75011

An old homeopathic chemist's shop is home to this unusual mix of tea room (serving organic teas), restaurant, bookshop, and retail store for organic products. It has become a sort of meeting place for students, young people, local artists, and anyone who wants to sit quietly or chat with friends. The character of the shop remains intact, and the original display cabinets now hold tins of tea. The main body of the earlier shop is filled with comfortable armchairs covered in velvet, where customers sit around low tables. Higher tables with matching chairs are arranged alongside one of the windows. How suitable that a drink so good for us is being served in

an old pharmacy where people once bought medicines and tonics to heal their ailments.

Items on the menu are all made with organic produce and include soups, salads, vegetable curries, and desserts such as chocolate mousse, fromage blanc, chestnut cream, and tiramisu. The certified organic teas include Chun Mee, Lung Ching, Kukicha, Gyokuro, Assam (Sewpur OP1), Darjeeling (Ambootia, Selimbong), Pai Mu Tan, Rooibos, Thé du Buddha, and Iced Lemon Tea.

• Tea room open Tues.- Wed., 10am-6pm, Thurs.-Sat., 10am-11pm, Sun., 10am-6pm. Closed Mon. • Nearest metro: Oberkampf (Lines 5, 9), République (Lines 3, 5, 8, 9, 11) • Tel: 01 43 38 04 99 • Major credit cards • Lunches, snacks, teas à la carte • E

Le Bar à Thé
Arrondissement: 12e
9 rue Ledru-Rollin, Paris 75012

Very much a local tea room, the mood here is youthful, easy-going, and relaxed. The style has been carefully planned to reflect a taste for natural products and materials. There is warm-colored wood and wicker (with chairs woven from banana leaves), rustic brickwork, and natural textures and tones as a backdrop for great food and really good teas. But there are light touches, too, in the twinkling lights that surround the bar, soft gauze curtains at the windows, and fun paintings around the room. Opposite is a pretty park with a bandstand and children playing, and when the shop spills out onto the pavement in warm weather, the view is gentle and calming. Young people love it here as easy jazz music and French songs play through the day.

Isabelle Cazet and her team chat amicably with their customers – who are more like friends – and the drink menu offers some unusual tea cocktails as an alternative to the excellent Darjeelings and oolongs. There's Paris Plage, a mixture of green tea, grapefruit juice, lemon syrup, and sugar syrup, or Happy, made with black tea, pineapple juice, vanilla, and lemon. A selection of iced teas are welcome on hot summer days, featuring blends of red fruits, almonds, bergamot, or peach with green and black teas. Hot teas are prepared in a paper filter inside a pretty teapot.

Teas include Lung Ching, Sencha Makoto, Genmaicha, Grand Oolong, Dung Ding, Silver Yun Cha, Puerh, Black Russian, Korean Forgotten Garden, Earl Grey Sencha, various flower teas (rose, violet, orange blossom, jasmine, cherry blossom), and various flavored teas including Kimono (peach and apricot) and Aladdin (ginger and flower petals).

• Bar-style tea room open Mon., 9am-4:30pm, Tue.-Sun., 9am-7:30pm in winter, 9am-8pm in summer • Nearest metro: Ledru-Rollin (Line 8) • Tel: 01 43 40 90 17 • Major credit cards • Breakfast, snacks, lunches, teas and tea cocktails à la carte • E

Les Cakes de Bertrand
Arrondissement: 9e
7 rue Bourdaloue, Paris 75009

Didier Bertrand keeps a quirky and very fresh artistic ambience in his shop by regularly changing the decor. Recent visitors found the little boudoir of a tea room decorated with a collage of fashion pictures, wallpaper designs, and music covers from the 1950s, with more of the same under glass table tops showing hair fashions, shoes, swimwear, and pretty frocks of that era. A glittering chandelier casts twinkling light over the room, and the glass shelves were decked with charming memorabilia. It seemed much like a stage set for The Nutcracker or Alice in Wonderland.

Cakes are the main event here, baked in the French style in loaf tins, so they are always rectangular rather than round. Didier is a master at blending different flavors and textures. He sells twenty or so creations including chocolate-orange, vanilla-orange, chocolate-almond, orange blossom, lemon, and preserved fruits. But the menu here is not only about sweet things. Order one of the salads for brunch or lunch, and you will be presented with a platter of farm-fresh grated celeriac and carrot, lentils, bulgar wheat, finely slivered fennel and parmesan with raisins and nuts, and freshly-baked savory tarts. Delicious!

Tea is brewed in a metal infuser, and the list includes Assam, Ceylon St. James, Darjeeling, Lapsang Souchong, Tarry Souchong, Sencha, Winter Sun (with orange and spice), and Red Kiss (with red fruits).

• Tea room with retail counter; open Tues.-Sat. 9:30am-7:30pm; brunch Sun., noon-6pm by reservation • Nearest metro: Notre-Dame-de-Lorette (Line 12) • Tel: 01 40 16 16 28 • Major credit cards • www.lescakesdebertrand.com • Breakfast, morning snacks, lunch and teas à la carte • E

Maxim's Salon de Thé

Arrondissement: 9e
Galeries Lafayette, magasin Coupole, 3rd floor
40 boulevard Haussman, Paris 75009

To find Maxim's, go up the escalator to the third floor in Galeries Lafayette (enjoy the ornate ceilings and balconies as you move), and wander to your left through the lingerie department. You'll soon find your way into the plush 1930s decor of a smart restaurant-tea room. The bright lipstick red and gold upholstery may make you gasp, and the sweet little chairs and tables will prove inviting. You can almost imagine yourself back in the heyday of big bands and art deco pizzaz.

The tea comes in elegant little muslin teabags inside a Maxim's teapot decorated with the salon's red logo. This little corner of fun and indulgence will restore you and send you off for another hour or two of shopping.

If you need sustenance during your morning shopping, choose a luxurious hot chocolate, coffee, or tea and indulge in delicious platefuls of bacon and eggs, fruit and pastries.

At lunchtime, try soup, pasta, or a club sandwich. For afternoon refreshment, there are cakes known as *souvenirs d'enfance* – memories of childhood! So, of course, you'll find chocolate cake, banana and nut cake, cherry cake, lemon and almond cake, apricot tart, macaroons, éclairs, mille feuilles slices, tiramisu, and melt-in-the-mouth sorbets and ice creams.

The tea comes in elegant little muslin teabags inside a Maxim's teapot decorated with the salon's red logo. This little corner of fun and indulgence will restore you and send you off for another hour or two of shopping. The tea list includes Darjeeling (Margaret's Hope), Grand Yunnan Imorial, Taiwanese Thé du Tigre (smoked), Sencha Superieur, Thé des Lords (Earl Grey with safflower petals), and Thé du Hammam (green tea with orange blossoms, rose petals, red fruits and green dates).

• Tea room open Mon.-Sat. 9:30am-6:30pm • Nearest metro: Chaussée d'Antin (Lines 7, 9), Opéra (Lines 3, 7, 8) • Tel: 01 40 16 18 23 • Major credit cards • Breakfast, lunch and teas à la carte • EE

Tea Basics

Black Tea
Black tea is fully-oxidized. Freshly-plucked green leaves are withered and then twisted or rolled to release and oxidize natural enzymes. Finally, the leaves are dried to become the familiar black leaf noted for its rich, full-bodied brew.

Blended Teas
Teas from a variety of estates are often combined to ensure a quality product under changing agricultural conditions. Flowers, fruit, herbs, spices, and scented or flavored oils may be added. Earl Grey is an example of a blended tea.

Compressed Tea
Green, black, and puerh teas are sometimes pressed into cakes and blocks of different shapes. These may be bowl-shaped, ball-shaped, flat and round, flat and triangular, flat and rectangular, or other combinations. For tea preparation, some of the cake is broken off and brewed in boiling water.

Green Tea
Freshly picked green tea leaves are steamed or panfired, rolled, and dried, not oxidized. Chinese green tea varieties tend to be more mellow than "grassy" Japanese teas.

Oolong Tea
This partially-oxidized tea traditionally comes from China and Taiwan. The flavors vary but are generally complex and gentle, sometimes fruity, and fragrant.

Puerh
Puerh teas are aged teas that are allowed to mature (sometimes for as along as 50 years) in order to develop an elemental, earthy flavor. The leaves are withered and then heaped in piles while still moist. The bacterium in the leaves causes a chemical reaction that gives the teas their distinctive aroma and taste. At the end of the process, the tea is dried and packed loose or pressed into cakes of different shapes and sizes. Puerh tea is said to be very good for you, especially if you have high cholesterol.

Rooibos
South African *Rooibos (ROY-boss)* or *Red Bush tea* is a caffeine-free herbal infusion, high in Vitamin C and antioxidant properties. It is thought to relieve insomnia, headaches, nausea, asthma, and allergies.

Tisane
Tisanes (tih-ZAHN) are made with herbs, flowers, fruit, roots, berries, bark, or the leaves of any plant other than *Camellia sinensis*. They do not contain caffeine. Peppermint, chamomile, and ginger are common herbal tisanes. Strawberries, apples, blueberries, and other dried fruits make delicious fruit infusions.

Water Temperature
Water temperature plays a very important role in the production of a good cup of tea. One easily remembered rule is: the lighter the tea, the cooler the water; the darker the tea, the hotter the water. These temperatures are recommended:

White tea and green teas - 165 - 185° F (73-85° C)
Oolong teas - 185-200° F (85-93° C)
Black and puerh teas - boiling

White Tea
White tea, which is prized (and often pricey) is made from young tea leaves and buds that are carefully picked and slowly dried, often in the sun. The curled buds have a silvery-white color and brew a straw-colored liquor. Originally grown in the Fujian province of China, white teas are now also produced in Sri Lanka and India. The pale liquor has a flavor that is soft, smooth, and slightly sweet.

L'Oisivethé

Arrondissement: 13e
1 rue Jean-Marie-Jégo, Paris 75013

Light, bright, and colorful, L'Oisivethé is quite charming. Outside, the walls on either side of the entrance are painted with tendrils of the tea plant and a tea caddy or two, plus a monkey, birds, butterflies, and teacups. This touch of fantasy and fun hints at the sunny, friendly atmosphere inside. The decor is light wood, with pretty table covers of tasseled Indian cotton. The walls are lined with shelves that display teapots, cups, bowls, pots of jam, chocolates, and brightly colored tins and packets of tea. Opposite is a tranquil little garden full of chestnut trees, a favorite haunt of the locals. The mood in this quiet corner of Paris is calm and neighborly.

The walls on either side of the entrance of L'Oisivethé are painted with tendrils of the tea plant and a tea caddy or two, plus a monkey, birds, butterflies, and teacups. This touch of fantasy and fun hints at the sunny, friendly atmosphere inside.

The foods offered are simple salads of fresh raw vegetables with cheeses or local ham, and for tea time, crumbles, yogurts, macaroons, and cakes. The tea list is impressive and contains teas that most people would not think of offering such as rare Chinese greens, as well as black teas from Nepal and Sichuan. There are fifteen classic teas, twelve flavored blends and eighteen L'Oisivethé specials. Among your choices are Darjeeling Bannockburn, Nepal Antu Valley, Ceylon St. James's, Grand Yunnan, Qimen Hao Ya, Sichuan, and iced green mint tea.

• Tea room open Tues.-Thurs. noon-7pm, Fri.-Sun., noon-8pm; brunch served noon-6pm. Closed in August • Nearest metro: Corvisart (Line 6) • Tel: 01 53 80 31 33 • www.loisivethe.free.fr • Lunches and teas à la carte • E

Rose-Thé

Arrondissement: 11e
104 avenue Ledru-Rollin, Paris 75011

Owned by Corinne and Mireille Gachelin, this totally charming tea room is a joy. It is pink but not overwhelmingly so; classic but with a modern twist; friendly, welcoming and warm but discreet. It has a demur, thoughtful mood but dares to hold exhibitions of modern art. The clients here are local residents – architects, artists, or friends meeting for a quiet conversation. There is a hint of expectation in the air, a sense that something wonderful or exciting may happen at any moment, that some famous personage may slip in to kiss the hand of one of the ladies. Rose-Thé's position close to so many places of interest on the eastern edge of the city (Le Marais, Place de la Bastille, and Père la Chaise cemetery) makes it the ideal place to have a revitalizing pot of tea.

At lunchtime, the menu offers deliciously fresh salads of feta cheese and tomatoes or avocado and prawns. You can get fish poached with fresh herbs or a grilled aubergine and tomato compote. These Parisians know how to turn wonderfully simple, fresh ingredients into a meal with flavors that linger in the memory. For dessert or at tea time, choose cherry clafoutis, lemon or fig tart, or apple crumble.

The loose leaf teas are measured into a large paper infuser bag and brewed in white porcelain teapots. The wide ranging list includes Yunnan Jade, Bi Lo Chun, Lung Ching, Ti Kuan Yin, Puerh Imperial, Yunnan Imperial, Grand Jasmine, and Rose de Beijing (green tea with red fruits). You'll also find Pivoine Blanche (White Peony or Pai Mu Tan), Japanese Sencha, Osmanthus Oolong, Lapsang Imperial, St. James's OP Ceylon, Darjeeling, Makaibari Organic, rose, vanilla, honey and orange, and Earl Grey Blue Flower.

• Mon.- Fri. 10am-7pm, Sat. 2:30-7pm • Nearest metro: Ledru-Rollin (Line 8) • Tel: 01 48 05 75 24 • Major credit cards • Breakfast, morning snacks, lunch and teas à la carte tea • E

Tea Mélodie
Arrondissement: 12e
72 boulevard de Picpus, Paris 75012

Traveling out to this quiet suburb to have tea in Georgios' *salon de thé* is well worth the effort because he is so nice and his waiters and waitresses are so friendly. It's the sort of shop that you leave vowing to come back one day. Georgios is Greek, not a nationality one associates with tea rooms, but he runs a successful business that is obviously a favorite spot for locals as it is often full of families and groups of ladies. The selection of teas isn't particularly exciting but it's adequate—and what is missing in the teas is amply made up for in the atmosphere.

An eclectic menu offers Nordic, Mexican, and Greek salads, home-made tarts and quiches, fruit crumbles, fromage blanc drizzled with fruit coulis, chocolate cakes, and specialties of the day. Teas include Ceylon, Darjeeling Princeton, Lapsang Souchong, Tsar Alexander Blend, Casablanca (green tea with mint), Marco Polo (China black tea with Chinese fruits and flowers), and Earl Grey.

• Open Mon.-Sat. 11am- 7pm. Closed in August • Nearest metro: Picpus (Line 6) • Major credit cards • Morning snacks, lunches and teas à la carte • E

Thé Troc
Arrondissement: 11e
52 rue Jean-Pierre-Timbaud, Paris 75011

Thé Troc is perfect for the bohemians, students, and revolutionaries amongst us – the sort of bookish, intellectual, hippy, slightly vagabond, and alternative gathering point that could only

exist in Paris. It has the air of a student sitting room. The windows and walls are covered with posters advertising events, books, ideas, performances; statues of Indian gods and Buddha sit on window sills and ledges, and books, newspapers, magazines, and journals lie on the tables. Little groups of students, music lovers, and young locals chat and laugh over their pots of tea.

There is an easy, take-us-or-leave-us sort of atmosphere where no one bothers you except to ask what you would like to drink and eat. Everything is slightly scruffy, but somehow that works to create an amusing, interesting, stimulating corner of the city. The shop section is dimly lit and packed full of vintage discs and second hand books. Ferid Kadour, the owner, and his son are always somewhere in the background, ready to advise on which tea to try and where to find a particular recording or publication that might interest you.

Thé Troc is perfect for the bohemians, students, and revolutionaries amongst us – the sort of bookish, intellectual, hippy, slightly vagabond, and alternative gathering point that could only exist in Paris.

The tea list is probably the most wide-ranging you will find anywhere and includes teas from unusual origins such as Vietnam, Malaysia, Laos, Thailand, Nepal, and Mozambique as well as China, India, Taiwan, Japan, Africa, and Sri Lanka. When you have chosen, the tea is delivered in an earthenware teapot, and you drink from a straight sided, Oriental-style, handleless cup.

• Bohemian tea room also selling books, music and bric-a-brac; open Mon.-Fri. 9:30am-8pm • Nearest metro: Parmentier (Line 3), Oberkampf (Lines 5, 9) • Tel: 01 43 55 54 80 • Major credit cards • Extensive list of loose teas from almost every tea producing country in the world, a few cakes • E

Musée de la vie Romantique
Arrondissement: 9e
16 rue Chaptal, Paris 75009

Since 1987, the Hotel Scheffer-Renan has housed the Musée de la Vie Romantique, bringing together objects, letters, paintings, jewelery, furniture and portraits associated with important intellectuals of 19th century Paris – George Sand, Chopin, Delacroix, Liszt, Rossini, and Dickens. Set on the lower slopes of the steep hill that climbs up to Montmartre, the elegant white and green house is in an area known as New Athens. The small but very pretty garden makes a perfect setting each summer for tea. The conservatory to the side of the house is cleverly transformed into a serving area and brewing counter. Visitors carry their trays out into the shade of the garden to relax, enjoy the lilac and roses, and sip their refreshing tea. It is a charming place to read or chat before or after wandering through the

house. The cakes and teas are supplied by Les Cakes de Bertrand.

Teas served are Fujiyama Green, Tibetan Secret flavored with lavender, Baikal, Green Long Tseng, Earl Grey, Ceylon Orange Pekoe, Lapsang Souchong, Mint tea, and Darjeeling Singbulli.

• Tea garden in the grounds of the museum, open from early May to mid-October, Tues.-Sun. 11:30am-5:30pm • Nearest metro: Saint-Georges (Line 12) • Tel: 01 55 31 95 67 • Cakes and teas à la carte • E

Shopping Sites for Tea Lovers

L'Empire des Thés
Arrondissement: 13e
101 Avenue d'Ivry, Paris, 75013

Set in an area studded with Vietnamese and Chinese restaurants and shops, this generously proportioned store offers a journey through Chinese tea. Here, you can learn from the kind and attentive assistants, browse the shelves of books on tea, and enjoy the visual beauty of the pots, bowls, trays, and brewing utensils from China and Taiwan.

The style of the shop is modern, light, and spacious. Minimalist shelving, neutral colors, and the sophisticated black of the tea tins appeals to a mixed clientele of those who know exactly what they want and those who are just beginning their adventure into Chinese teas.

The tea list is extensive, offering more than 160 different varieties from numerous provinces. There are white teas from Fujian; yellow teas from Anhui, Guangdong and Hunan; green teas from eleven provinces including Anhui, Zhejiang, and Yunnan; and oolongs from Fujian, Guangdong, and Taiwan. You'll find red teas (what we call black teas) from Anhui and Fujian, smoked teas from five provinces, seven puerh teas, display teas, and teas from Vietnam, Japan, India, Africa, and Russia. There are about 45 flavored teas that include classic jasmines, rose, and osmanthus flavors. To taste any of the teas, take a seat near the window at one of the carved wooden tables and watch the world go by as you sip your chosen brew. A visit here guarantees that you will leave knowing more than when you arrived.

Set in an area studded with Vietnamese and Chinese restaurants and shops, this generously proportioned store offers a journey through Chinese tea.

• Tea retail store with tasting area, open Tues.-Sun., 11am-8pm • Nearest metro: Tolbiac (Line 7) • Tel: 01 45 85 66 33 • www.empiredesthes.com

Lafayette Gourmet

Arrondissement: 9e
48 boulevard Haussmann, Paris 7509

This food section of Galeries Lafayette is in a separate building from the main department store (where Maxims tea salon is on the 3rd floor). Walk west along boulevard Haussman until you find the entrance. Up on the first floor, Hédiard has a counter set out with their very bright red tins of loose leaf teas, and a few other tea companies have their products in the same area. Take the staircase down to street level, and in one corner a signpost will point you to the Comptoir de Thé, a very stylish tea area where you may sample the teas that sit in glass pots on their little night-lights to keep warm. The teas are from the Thé Indar Compagnie Coloniale, a tea company selling loose organic teas and infusions and muslin teabags.

• Department store with small tea retail counters in various locations, open Mon.-Sat., 9:30am-8:30pm; Thurs. open until 9pm • Nearest metro: Chaussée d'Antin (Lines 3, 7, 9), Opéra (Lines 3, 7, 8) • Tel: 01 42 82 36 40 • www.galerieslafayette.com

Directly across the street from Galeries Lafayette stands the grand Opéra Garnier. It was built for Napoleon II in 1875 and is the setting for Phantom of the Opera. It is no longer home to the Paris Opéra but it is open for ballet, occasional concerts, and a fascinating tour.

Lafayette Maison

Arrondissement: 9e
Boulevard Haussman, Paris 75009

Galeries Lafayette today fills three separate buildings, and Lafayette Maison is on the opposite side of the road from the main store between boulevard Hassmann and rue Charras. This is where to come if you want to buy table linens, cutlery, lamps, furniture, gourmet food, and tea. Mariage Frères has a counter in the basement, selling a small selection of their most popular teas and other products. On the ground floor is a pretty selection of oriental tea wares, earthenware pots, cups, and bowls. So if you haven't found the right tea things elsewhere on your travels around Paris, browse through this department.

• Home store section of Galeries Lafayette; open Mon.-Sat. 9:30am-8:30pm; Thurs., open until 9pm • House and table wares and some teas and food • Nearest metro: Chaussée d'Antin (Lines 3, 7, 9), Opéra (Lines 3, 7, 8) • Tel: 01 42 82 36 40 • www.galerieslafayette.com

Old England - Fortnum & Mason

Arrondissement: 9e
12 boulevard des Capucines or 2 rue Scribe Paris 75009

Old England is a department store dedicated to selling very British products including Burberry, Dunhill, Wedgwood, Floris, and, of course, tea from Fortnum and Mason. There are entrances to the store from two streets, and the tea section is tucked into the corner on the ground floor. You won't find the entire Fortnum and Mason range, but there is a good selection of teas, biscuits, Wedgwood cups and saucers, chrome and glass teapots, mugs with fitted infusers, chocolates,

hampers, chutneys, marmalades, jams, lemon curds, honey, and whiskey.

Teas include Darjeeling BOP, Assam TGFOP, Ceylon OP, Breakfast Blend, Afternoon Blend, Earl Grey Classic (a blend of China and Ceylon with bergamot), Queen Ann, Jasmine, Irish Breakfast (Assam and Kenya), Royal Blend (India and Ceylon), Lapsang Souchong, and various flavored teas.

• Fortnum & Mason counter inside Old England department store, open Mon.-Sat. 10:30am-7pm. Closed every Monday in August. • Nearest metro: Opéra (Lines 3, 7, 8) • Tel: 01 47 42 81 99 • Major credit cards • www.fortnumandmason.co.uk

Le Parti du Thé
Arrondissement: 11e
34 rue Faidherbe, Paris 75011

Pierre Lebrun opened this stunning little store in 2005, and it is an impressive part of the wave of amazingly well-stocked tea stores owned and run by enlightened tea aficionados like him. Before you enter the shop, enjoy the window display which Pierre always decorates according to the season or current event.

As you walk in, stop and admire the clever way in which the teas and tea wares are arranged around the shop. The bulk teas are stored in large bright orange tins stacked on turntables behind the counter, and samples of the different leaf are divided into categories (white, green, oolong, black, puerh), color-coded, and displayed in gleaming glass tubes set in racks that lean at an angle against the walls. It almost has the feel of a very modern pharmacy – highly suitable given all tea's recognized health benefits.

Pierre Lebrun opened Le Parti du Thé in 2005, and it is an impressive part of the wave of amazingly well-stocked tea stores owned and run by enlightened tea aficionados like him. It almost has the feel of a very modern pharmacy – highly suitable given all tea's recognized health benefits.

Elegant plinths arranged around the shop hold lovely caddies and teapots, bowls and guywans, scoops and infusers. Customers are treated to regular tasting events in the shop, and Pierre and fellow shop keepers in the same area have recently set up the Association Village Faidherbe, which organizes street markets to sell a range of quality products in a lively neighborhood atmosphere. There is real passion here and a determination to spread the word about tea to anyone who steps into this delightful shop.

Pierre sells a wide selection (260 different varieties) of top quality teas including Lung Ching, Assam 2nd Flush (Golden Doomni), Darjeelings (1st Flush Margaret's Hope, Darjeeling Wonder Oolong, Sikkim TGFOP), Tanzanian Chivanjee, Chinese Oolong, Puerh, and Kai Hua Long Ting.

• Tea retail store open Mon. 1:30-7:30pm, Tues.-Fri. 10:30am-7:30pm, Sat. 10am-8pm • Nearest metro: Faidherbe-Chaligny (Line 8) • Tel: 01 43 72 42 04 • Major credit cards • Loose leaf teas, brewing equipment and tea gifts

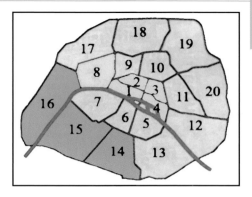

The Eiffel Tower
and Beyond

Arrondissements 14, 15, 16

Standing on the terraces at Trocadero, your view will capture *La Tour Eiffel* and its parks that stretch away to the southeast. The charming mix of quieter streets and small neighborhood squares brings moments of calm content away, for just a short while, from the city's wildly beating heart.

Carette
Arrondissement: 16e
4 place du Trocadéro, Paris 75016

Carette is one of those typical street café-brasseries that always have customers sitting at the tables ranged out on the pavement, no matter what the weather. This is a friendly, lively café with plenty of regulars who are greeted with a loud *bonjour* from the staff, plus a colorful mix of tourists, shoppers and locals. Inside there is plenty of room if the tables outside are packed. On the way in, stop to cast your eye over the array of cakes and pastries

that includes all the usual religieuses, opéra chocolate slices, rum babas, mille feuilles slices, pain au chocolat, and macaroons. The waitresses dress in classic black and white, are pleasant and helpful to everyone, and seem to enjoy scurrying in and out with heavy trays of drinks, snacks, and full meals. Loose leaf teas are brewed inside a metal infuser that sits inside the silver pot until you choose to remove it.

Teas include Ceylon, China smoked, Grand Souchong, Earl Grey, Jasmine, Darjeeling, Japanese green, green mint tea, and Cornflower Blend.

• Typical Parisian brasserie serving good tea and a range of snacks and pastries, open every day 7am; closes at midnight in summer, 11pm in winter • Nearest metro: Trocadéro (Lines 6, 9) • Tel: 01 47 27 98 85 • Reservations recommended • Major credit cards • www.carette-paris.com • Breakfast, brunch, lunch, tea by the pot, savory and sweet dishes à la carte, dinner • E

Thé Cool
Arrondissement: 16e
10 rue Jean-Boulogne, Paris 75016

Tucked around the corner at the far end of rue Jean-Boulogne, Thé Cool is fun and welcoming. Michèle Laporta and Marie-Claude Mercier have been here for 20 years or so, serving tea and looking after a lively regular clientele. The mood is light and bright, relaxed and easy, the sort of place that makes you feel really alive. Drop in for lunch, and tuck into a quiche or tart, a healthy salad or a boiled egg or two. For dessert, choose from the selection of cakes, scones, fruit crumbles, various flavors of fromage blanc, and chocolate charlotte – all excellent.

More than 30 different teas are offered, including various Ceylons, Darjeelings and Assams, Douchka (Russian blend), Grand Oolong, Superior English Blend (Indian, Ceylon, China), Jasmine, Yunnan, Caravan Blend, Lapsang Souchong, and green mint tea.

• Tea room, open Mon.-Sat., noon–7pm, Sun. 11am-6pm • Nearest metro: La Muette (Line 9) • Tel: 01 42 24 69 13 • Major credit cards • Lunches and teas à la carte • EE

At Thé Cool, choose a dessert from their enticing selection of cakes, scones, fruit crumbles, cheesecakes, or fruit tarts.

Shopping Sites for Tea Lovers

Boissier
Arrondissement: 16e
184 avenue Victor Hugo, Paris 75016

A bright blue theme runs throughout the Boissier store and lifts the spirit as soon as you walk through the door. Counters and shelves are laden with blue packets, boxes, and tins of sweets, chocolates, jams, and teas. There is a hint of theatrics in the way the shop is arranged. Round blue boxes that resemble mini hat boxes are suspended from the ceiling or climb atop each other in precarious stacks. Small pink pouches, with who knows what mouth-watering delicacies inside, dangle temptingly alongside. Lidded glass urns stand in ranks filled with handmade chocolates and bonbons. Cheeky moustached tin *chocolatiers* stand in their white aprons on the counter top, and shiny packets of little cakes and biscuits invite you to pick them up and take them home. Loose leaf teas are stored in large round blue drums and are measured out for customers or sold in 100 gram packets. Boissier was founded in 1826, originally in boulevard des Capucines and has been here in avenue Victor Hugo for more than 50 years. Perhaps it will still be here in another 50.

Teas include Boissier Blend (tea from China and Ceylon flavored with citrus fruits and lavender), Darjeeling, Ceylon Flowery Orange Pekoe, Earl Grey, and Caramel.

• Confectionery and bakery selling some loose leaf teas, open Mon.-Sat. 10am-7pm • Nearest metro: Rue de la Pompe (Line 9) • Tel: 01 45 03 50 77 • Major credit cards • Confectionery, cakes, chocolates, teas

La Compagnie des Thés
Arrondissement: 15e
12 rue Violet, Paris 75015

There are strong connections between this small, successful, neighborhood store and Russian tea and nobility. The first important link is that Joe Canet, one of the owners, previously worked for Kusmi tea company. In the 1920s, Kusmi launched a shop in London and a tea room in Paris under the name Compagnie des Thés that sold the best Russian blend teas anywhere in the world. When Kusmi started trading again in Paris, Joe decided to take the Compagnie name and relaunch it here in this quiet suburb. The other fascinating Russian connection is that Joe's partner, Prince Orlov, is the grandson of one of the Romanov princesses. So here we have an interesting history of tea in Russia and Paris via London and a company still trading excellent teas today. Bright red and black packaging seem very suitable, given the heritage, as well as the actual teas. The shop offers Tetsubin teapots in all sizes and colors, caddies, tins, measures and scoops, infusers, teapot stands, treasure teas, trays, biscuits, and cocoa.

Teas include Ceylon OP, Windsor Blend (Assam and Darjeeling blend), Tarry Souchong, Ti Kuan Yin, Yunnan Imperial, Yunnan Green Mao Feng, Darjeeling First Flush, 1878 Blend (with bergamot and lemon), Special Orlov blend (with citrus fruits and spices), and Yoggi Tchaï (Indian tea with spices).

• Small tea retail shop, open Mon.- Sat., 10:30am-8pm • Nearest metro: Dupleix (Line 6) • Tel: 01 45 78 10 64 • Major credit cards • Loose teas, tea brewing equipment, tea gifts

L'Empire des Thés
Arrondissement:14e
69 rue du Montparnasse, Paris, 75014

This is a smaller version of the store in avenue d'Ivry and sells the same vast offering of teas from all of China's tea producing provinces and from around the world. The space is more limited but the shop still manages to create an atmosphere of adventure and enticing oriental attractions. The same large black tins hold the

(Continued on page 100)

"The shop is a little away from the center of the city, but Sandrine Letestu attracts a steady stream of regular local customers who enjoy the friendly, homey atmosphere and the easy jazz music that plays in the background."

L'Infinithé
Arrondissement: 15e
8 rue Desnouettes, Paris 75015

Sandrine Letestu owns and runs this tiny tea room with a flair for serving excellent foods and for enthusing her customers about the teas she serves. The shop is a little away from the center of the city, but she attracts a steady stream of regular local customers who enjoy the friendly, homey atmosphere and the easy jazz music that plays in the background.

The soothing voices of Stacey Kent and Diana Krall fill the air while customers enjoy one of Sandrine's 30 or so well-chosen teas. She specializes in flavored teas that include green leaf flavored with almond, mint and rose, jasmine, Moroccan nana mint, cherry, rhubarb and strawberry, and black teas blended with cinnamon, almond, coconut, hazelnut and vanilla, maracuja with grapefruit and strawberry. For lunch, the menu offers vegetable quiches and tarts with a tomato coulis,

steamed salmon fillet or smoked salmon quiche. Desserts include crumbles, chocolate mousse, or fromage blanc with nuts, fruits and honey. Brunch is a satisfying selection of eggs, smoked salmon, fresh fruits, salads, little sandwiches, toast, and cakes. The set tea includes a pot of tea with either a pastry or a cake with orange marmalade, or a serving of hot toast with butter and jam.

Teas include Darjeeling Jungpana, Ceylon St. James OP, China smoked, Pai Mu Tan, Genmaicha, Sencha, Russian Caravan, Oolong Fancy, Earl Grey, Tarry Souchong, Yunnan, Puerh, Lung Ching, 15 flavored teas, and various infusions.

• Tea room open Tues.-Fri. noon-6pm, Sat. 12:30pm-3pm. Closed Sunday. • Nearest metro: Convention (Line 12) • Tel: 01 40 43 14 23 • Major credit cards • Morning snacks, lunch, brunch, set tea, and tea à la carte • EE

loose leaf, the counter and shelves are stacked with teapots, books, jams, packets of little biscuits and sweets to eat with tea, tea filters, Gong Fu trays and utensils; in fact everything that you would find in a tea store in Taiwan or China. What always makes a visit to shops like this worthwhile is the willingness of the assistants to offer advice and information and to help us learn more about the art of Chinese tea.

The tea list includes four different grades of Lung Ching, seven puerhs, thirteen oolongs (what the French call blue-green tea) from Fujian province and several others from Guangdong and Taiwan, and teas flavored with forest strawberries, mango and lychee, cardamom, orange blossom, ginger, caramel and vanilla, and jasmine.

• Tea retail store with tasting area, open Tues.-Sun., 11am-8pm • Nearest metro: Edgar Quinet (Line 6) • Tel: 01 45 85 66 33 • www.empiredes-thes.com • Loose leaf teas, tea foods, brewing equipment, tea gifts

Le Palais des Thés
Arrondissement: 16e
21 rue de l'Annonciation, Paris 75016

Like other branches of this very enterprising and exciting tea company, this shop is full of wonderful products. And also as elsewhere, don't be afraid to ask for advice, help, or information. This company specializes in passing on whatever they know and making it fun to learn.

Through their direct contact with the plantations they buy from, they are able to find unusual and less readily available teas. They also make a difference in the lives and conditions of the workers who grow and manufacture the teas by ensuring that legal requirements of health, safety, and pay are adhered to. At the same time, they become involved in any environmental issues such as deforestation and water supplies.

Take advantage of the knowledge and expertise here. Enjoy finding out more before selecting from more than 200 teas from all over the world.

• Tea retail store, open Mon. 10am–6pm, Tues.-Sat., 10am-7pm. Closed Sunday. • Nearest metro: Passy (Line 6) • Tel: 01 45 25 51 52 • http://palais-prod.cvf.fr/eng (Excellent website) • Retail store selling loose leaf teas, cakes, storage tins, candles, tea filters, fruits in syrup, chestnuts

Le Palais des Thés
Arrondissement: 14e
25 rue Raymond-Losserand, Paris 75014

This is another exciting Palais des Thés store that attracts a steady stream of dedicated tea drinkers. The products are extremely attractive, the amount of knowledge and expertise astonishing, and the atmosphere is fun, friendly, and helpful. The colorful window and shop displays attract newcomers who find it hard to resist the bright, modern, exciting colors and the buzz that each shop enjoys. Palais des Thés shops are never over-crowded with goods but are tastefully arranged to set things off at their best and allow customers to see exactly what is on offer. The colors of the decor work with the colors of the stylish Japanese Tetsubin teapots and the streamlined gift boxes, the smart packets and tins of tea, and the sample area where shoppers can smell the different aromas and examine the leaves. The concept is very successful, and the company has stores in Japan, Brussels, and Beverly Hills as well as in other major cities in France.

Choose from over 200 teas of all varieties – white, green, oolong, black, smoked, flavored, decaffein-ated, puerh and compressed.

• Tea retail store, open Mon.-Sat. 10am-7pm. Closed Sunday • Nearest metro: Pernety (Line 13) • Tel: 01 43 21 97 97 • http://palais-prod.cvf.fr/eng (Excellent website) • Loose leaf teas, gingerbreads, tea sweets, brewing equipment, cups and saucers, candles, tea box sets.

La Route du Thé
Arrondissement: 15e
2 rue de Mademoiselle, Paris 75015

The owners of La Route du Thé have chosen their locations well, opening shops in suburbs

Panthéon Bouddique at Musée Guimet
Arrondissement: 16e
Hôtel Heidelbach, 19 avenue Iéna, Paris 75116

Part of the Guimet National Museum of Asiatic Art, this delightful collection of Japanese and Chinese Buddhas and Buddhist art is not housed in the main Guimet museum but in a small hotel just round the corner along avenue Iéna. Emile Guimet (1836-1918) was a wealthy industrialist who loved to travel, and when he returned from a trip to Japan in 1876 he brought back a number of exceptional works that became the foundation of his museum. In this separate collection are Buddhist paintings and sculptures dating back to the 6th century.

The art is impressive, but the charm of this part of the museum is the little garden and Japanese tea house set at the back of the building. In recognition of the link between tea and Buddhism, the tea house was designed by Professor Masao Nakamura of the Institute of Japanese Art and built by the best Japanese carpenters. The tranquil garden that surrounds it is designed to create the peace and calm required for the preparation of the mind before participation in the tea ceremony. Giant stalks of bamboo cast soft shadows over the stepping stones and statue of Buddha, and wooden walkways traverse a large pond that adds its stillness to the sense of serenity. The traditional Tea Ceremony is held here on certain days; telephone to find out more or to arrange a group visit.

• Gallery of Japanese and Chinese Buddhist artifacts; Japanese garden and tea house open every day, 10am–5:45pm; closed Tues. Garden open every day, 1-5pm; closed Tues. • Nearest metro: Boissière (Line 6), Iéna (Line 9) • Tel: 01 56 523 53 00 • Free entry

where other tea shops have not ventured. Here to the southwest of the city's center, there is little competition for such an excellent range of more than 300 teas from almost every possible origin. Ask the assistant in the shop for advice, as staff members are always eager to please and to talk about the teas and other products. If you are interested in jasmine teas, ask what the difference is between the 16 varieties and grades. If you have a taste for Darjeelings, discuss the attributes of the different flushes from 20 or more gardens. Assam is well represented in this shop, and there are both large and broken leaf grades from a dozen different estates. If you are interested in unusual compressed teas, choose from round cakes, bricks, compressed puerhs, and mini Tuo Cha flavored with rose.

• Tea retail store, open Tues.-Sat. 11am-7pm • Closed Sun.-Mon. • Nearest metro: Félix Faure (Line 8) • Major credit cards • www.larouteduthe. com • Loose leaf teas and teabags, brewing equipment, decorative objects, tea gifts

Thé ô Dor
Arrondissement: 16e
28 rue des Sablons, Paris 75016

Nadia Leleu is totally passionate about her shop and her teas. There is nothing of the old fashioned image of tea here. Everything is vibrant, alive, full of interest and inspiration. Nadia established her business in this former dairy and the old wall tiles still show a handsome brown cow grazing in the green fields of rural France at the beginning of the last century. Despite working in such a small space, she has filled the shop with an amazing number of colors, aroma and products, and the key word here is seduction! Teapots from Japan and China are pink and sky blue, bright crimson and jade green, teas are packed in bright shiny packets and tins, gleaming jars hold zingy marmalades and jams full of plump fruit, candles in

Nadia Leleu established her business in this former dairy and the old wall tiles still show a handsome brown cow grazing in the green fields of rural France at the beginning of the last century.

gift tins smell divine, generous cylindrical black tins hold all the loose leaf teas, and lids are happily removed temporarily to allow customers to breathe in and savor the wonderful aromas. It's a treasure trove of lovely tempting things.

• Small tea retail shop, open Mon.-Fri. 9:30am-7:30pm, Sat. 9.30am-8pm • Nearest metro: Trocadéro (Lines 6, 9), Rue de la Pompe (Line 9) Tel: 01 45 05 25 98 • Tea retail shop selling tea, candles, soaps, jams, bath salts and other gifts • www.theodor.fr • Loose leaf teas, brewing equipment, candles, soaps, caddies, seasonings, tea gifts

Thés Emmanuel Laffarge
Arrondissement: 14e
59 rue Sarrette, Paris 75014

Nothing has changed inside this shop for about 50 years. It has recently changed hands but the previous owner, Norbert, continues to work alongside the younger Saida who has taken over, and the decor and stock remain as before. The shop is very much a local corner shop selling all sorts of unusual organic food, diet and medicinal products that are popular with those who care about how they eat and drink, how they look, and how they feel.

There is a vision here of how we should care about our food, ourselves and each other. It's a place where people offer advice and information, chat and exchange news. It's the sort of shop you wish was more available every time you find yourself in a huge supermarket where there's never anyone to ask and you can rarely find unusual products.

The teas are displayed in large tins at the far left side of the shop where there is plenty of room to browse before deciding. Choose from a wide selection that includes Darjeeling Goomtee First Flush, Ceylon, Assam, Formosa Oolong, Lung Ching, Gunpowder, Sichuan, Keemun and Grand Yunnan.

• Tea retail shop also selling organic and homeopathic products; open Tues.-Sat. 10am-1pm and 3:30-8pm • Nearest metro: Porte d'Orléans (Line 4) Tel: 01 45 40 73 09 • Major credit cards • Loose leaf teas, health foods

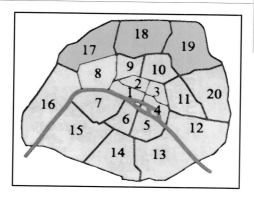

The Northern Hills

Arrondissements 17, 18, 19

Explore the far perimeter of the city to the
northwest, climb the upper slopes of the
steep hill crowned by the Sacré Coeur and
you will encounter small highways and by-
ways, historic cemeteries, church squares
and the haunts of painters and poets.
Do not hurry – if you do you will miss
the very essence of the place.

Au Vieux Four
Arrondissement: 19e
83 rue de Crimée, Paris 75019

All the original features are still evident inside
this excellent family bakery where Véronique
Mauclerc and her mother, Agnès, bake,
sell, and serve the most delicious breads
(30 or so different types and flavors),
croissants, brioches, fruit tarts, flans, gingerbreads, pizzas, and savory quiches.

There is a very homey sense of nostalgia
and history here. The wall tiles, large
framed mirror, and generous counter and
racks that hold the freshly baked loaves
are original, as is the vast oven at the
back where all these irresistible products
are baked. The counter is attractively arranged with stacks of baguettes in wicker

baskets, and glass shelves display madeleines, apple tarts, little biscuits and fruit tartlets. There are a few tables where customers can rest a while and savor some of the house specialties. The atmosphere is very much of a neighborhood bakery where locals pop in to get their croissants for breakfast, their bread for lunch, and a fancy gâteau or a fruit flan for dessert at dinner or Sunday lunch. Teas include Jasmine, Rose, Ceylon Green Fields, Finest Earl Grey, Chun Mee, Yunnan, and Babouchka (Russian blend).

• Bakery and tea room, open Mon. and Thurs.-Sun. 8am-8pm. Closed Tues. & Wed.• Nearest metro: Botzaris (Line 7bis), Laumière (Line 5) • Tel: 01 42 40 64 55 • E

India Kala
Arrondissement: 18e
57 rue Ramey, Paris 75018

When Bérengère Gazielly first traveled to India in 2001, she discovered such a wealth of art,

crafts, and culture that she decided to create a small tea salon and boutique dedicated to offering Parisians some of the treasures she had found. She trades only with companies around the world who work within the Fair Trade ethic. The little shop that she opened in 2004 sells spices from India and Madagascar, olive oil from Palestine, preserves from Benin, quinoa from Bolivia, coffee from Tanzania, chocolate from Costa Rica, dried banana chips from the Philippines, fruit juice from Laos, sugar from Ecuador,

India Kala is the only Fair Trade tea shop in Paris.

and organic teas from India. This is, in fact, the only Fair Trade tea shop in Paris.

The tables at which customers sit to take tea are surrounded by handmade objects and collectibles from India – furniture, picture frames, silver jewelry, pretty stationery, wooden toys, printed fabrics, and pottery. The walls are saffron, the tables and counter terracotta red, the atmosphere warm, artisanal, and welcoming. Local people spend hours here, and the no smoking policy means that everyone can be comfortable. Mothers bring their children, young people come back frequently, and families sit together for brunch or tea. The organic teas are brewed in infusers or bags with filtered water, and the list includes Nilgiri Oothu, Assam Banasparty, Dooars Putharjhora, Darjeeling Seeyok Spring Flush, Selimbong oolong, Chai, and Jasmine Spice.

• Indian-themed tea room, open Tues. 3-8:30pm, Wed.-Sat., 11:30am-8:30pm, Sun. 11am-7:30pm • Nearest metro: Jules Joffrin (Line 12), Marcadet-Poissoniers (Line 4, 12) • Tel: 01 42 52 47 69 • Seating is limited so reservations are recommended • www.India-kala.com • Indian foods, Fair Trade foods and beverages from around the world, crafts and tea wares • E

Le Stübli

Arrondissement: 17e
11 rue Poncelet, Paris, 75017

Proprietor Gerhard Weber brought his pâtisserie skills from Germany to France and set up business in this colorful gastronomic street. His shop is in a foodie's heaven, with an entire street given over to specialist shops selling wine, cheese, bread, fish, pastries, and chocolates, plus a street market selling the most colorful array of vegetables, fruits, shellfish, and fish anyone could hope to find anywhere. It is truly a feast for the eyes! Everywhere you look, there are large round artichokes, shiny plump tomatoes, a dozen or more different types of mushrooms and fungi, melons, apples, grapes, leeks, bunches of herbs, salad leaves, fat pink and white heads of garlic, and huge trays covered with crushed ice on top of which sit crayfish, prawns, lobsters and crabs. You can do an entire day or week's worth of shopping here. But don't go away without stopping for tea and a cake at Le Stübli. Gerhard is utterly charming, gentle, and kind, and his shop is filled with delicious things.

Proprietor Gerhard Weber brought his pâtisserie skills from Germany to France and set up business in this colorful gastronomic street.

Tea is served upstairs where the theme is Black Forest. The teas include Ceylon, Darjeeling, Lapsang Souchong, Earl Grey, Russian Blend, and Stübli blend (Earl Grey with Lotus).

• Pâtisserie open Tues.-Sat. 9am-7:30pm, Sun. 9am-1pm. Tea room open Tues.-Sat. 9am-6:30pm, Sun. 9am-12:30pm • Nearest metro: Ternes (Line 2) • Tel: 01 42 27 81 86 • Major credit cards • www.stubli.com • Wonderful cakes and pastries, breakfast, lunch and tea à la carte • E

Thé de Yi

Arrondissement: 17e
27 rue Bayen, Paris 75017

In 2003, Dai Yan Ying from Hangzhou in China opened this very attractive and interesting store. She now enjoys the patronage of local tea lovers who often visit to buy loose tea for home brewing. They also tend to sit awhile to enjoy a cup of tea and a dish of steamed Chinese pasta or a plateful of sashimi or sushi, filet of fish steamed with green tea and ginger, sweet Chinese dumplings with rice, and black sesame seed sweetmeats.

The area including rue Poncelet and rue Bayen is home to one of the city's most colorful street markets where food is art!

Customers sit at square Chinese, carved-wood tables, and all around are large mirrors, clothes, table wares, tea wares, and books for sale. Dai Yan has planned everything very carefully, and although one might expect to have her thoughtfully chosen China oolongs brewed in an unglazed, earthenware Yixing pot, she uses a Japanese iron Tetsubin pot because she says the tea brews more quickly and stays hotter inside. *Yi* means art and the selection and presentation of the teas and other seductive range of goods on sale is indeed artful. Dai Yan loves to help and is kind and gentle with her customers who can drink an exquisite Ti Kuan Yin from Fujian province, a rare yellow tea from Jushan, or a Tuo Cha (a little compressed nest) flavored with rice.

Teas include Jushan Yellow Needles, Ti Kuan Yin Iron Goddess and Gold Goddess, Yin Zhen Silver Needles, Bi Lo Chun, rice flavored Tuo Cha, Qimen Hong, and Red Tea blended with toasted grains.

• Chinese tea retail shop and tea room, open Mon.-Sat. 10am-6:30pm • Nearest metro: Ternes (Line 2) • Tel: 01 45 74 16 18 • Major credit cards • Loose leaf teas, tea brewing equipment and table wares, morning snacks, lunch and teas à la carte • EE

Shopping Sites for Tea Lovers

Bonthés et Accessoires

Neighborhood: 18e
157 rue Marcadet, Paris 75018

Shopping for tea here is like paying a visit to a magician. Morad Ounnaghi's total dedication to tea and his passion for informing, instructing, sharing, and advising fills you with a sense of well-being and tempts you to stand chatting for longer than you realize. This wonderful little shop gives the appearance of being tiny from the outside, but inside it is an entire world of treats, tastes, smells, gifts, and Morad's generous-hearted kindness. He has an amazing collection of music CDs under the counter and asks you what you would like to listen to while you decide what to buy – Mozart or Brahms, French ballads or opera. Your time here becomes part shopping and part concert. Along with teas, Morad sells jams and honeys, candies and Turkish Delight, oriental bowls, teapots, scoops, filters, books, and baskets.

The list of more than 200 teas includes black, green, white, oolong, puerh, compressed, and flavored varieties from China, Japan, India, Sri Lanka, Nepal, Taiwan, Kenya, Mauritius, and South Africa. Morad offers special house blends and classic favorites such as Irish Blend, Big Ben Breakfast tea, various Earl Greys, and exotic blends flavored with wild strawberries, dates, peaches and figs, or mango, coconut, and ginger.

• Tea retail shop, open Tues.-Sun. 10:30am-1:30pm and 3-8pm • Nearest metro: Lamarck-Caulaincourt (Line 12) • Tel: 01 55 79 76 52 • Major credit cards • Loose leaf teas, sweets, pots, bowls, measures, caddies and tea gifts

A Walk through Montmartre

This fascinating and colorful hilltop neighborhood encompasses all that is sacred and profane about Paris. Tourists often go immediately to Sacré Coeur, the second most visited church in Paris, and miss all the history that surrounds it. Budget at least a half day to wander the narrow streets and peek into the homes, cafés, and shops where famous artists and poets found inspiration a century ago.

Begin your journey at the Blanche Metro station, directly in front of the Moulin Rouge. Head north up Rue Lepic and you will pass the homes of Van Gogh and Toulousse-Lautrec. Further along the way, you will recognize Picasso's studio at the intersection of Rue D'Orchampt and Rue Ravignan.

As you continue your climb toward the top of this highest hill in Paris, you encounter simple outdoor cafés, bakeries, and bookstores. There is even a small hillside vineyard just a block from the house where Renoir lived. You cannot get lost if you continue climbing higher toward your goal. The bright shining marble domes of Sacré Coeur are your guide.

Unlike the often noisy Notre Dame, this quiet sanctuary serves as a peaceful respite for pilgrims of all faiths. Sit awhile and rest your soul. Later, you can join hundreds of fellow travelers as you take time to photograph Paris from the front steps. The endless stairs to the right lead to the Anvers Metro station.

Versailles

Once an insignificant village, the town today is dominated by the grandeur and splendor of the château that was home to Louis XIV. The arrival of the royal court in the 17th century led to the gradual development of new houses and shops, monuments, parks and gardens. Today the streets are as busy as any modern city.

Gaulupeau
44 rue de la Paroisse, Versailles 78000

Versailles is dominated by the presence and style of its château. Wide roads sweep from one part of the town to another, and period houses and apartments mirror the architecture of the late 17th and early18th centuries when the town developed under King Louis XIV. Shops are housed in elegant buildings that developed through the reigns of Louis XV and Louis XVI. Gaulupeau is an excellent example of how the royal residents colored the tastes of the locals as they mirrored the designs of château rooms in their own interiors. The business was established in 1769 as Pâtisserie Notre-Dame, and the gilded mirrors remain, along with the trompe l'oeil ceilings with blue sky and clouds, the creamy pink walls, and the classic boudoir intimacy. Small round marble tables are perfect for two, and hushed conversations keep visitors guessing as to their content and importance.

Lunchtime brings salmon quiche, Roquefort tart, omelettes, and hot rice dishes with salmon and a cream sauce. Dessert may be selected from the counter at the front of the shop, which is laden with traditional

rum babas, mille feuilles, cherry clafoutis, chocolate mousse, meringues, and macaroons.

Teas are brewed in paper filters and include Earl Grey, Darjeeling, Grand Yunnan, Imperial Gold (smoked tea with jasmine flowers), Jasmine, Mint Green tea, Sencha Fukuyu, and Chocolate flavored tea (black China tea flavored with dark chocolate).

• Tea room and pâtisserie open Tues.-Sat. 8am-7:30pm, Sun. 8am-6:30pm • Nearest station: Versailles mainline station • Tel: 01 39 50 01 63 • Major credit cards • Breakfast, lunch, teas à la carte, retail cakes and pastries • E

Le Parnasse
4 rue Andre Chenier, Versailles 78000

The square around the market in Versailles is full of restaurants and brasseries, so if you are looking for somewhere a little more oriented towards tea, go to Le Parnasse. It is named after the 19th century group of poets that counted Théophile Gautier, Gustave Flaubert, Rimbaud, Mallarmé, and Verlaine amongst their number. You are in romantic company as you relax, on warm days, at a table outside on the pavement. In cooler weather, choose a table inside where soft yellow walls and pale flagstones create an ambience of quiet calm. This salon does not have the style or panache of the Parisian tea rooms, but you will get a better cup here than at the other neighboring establishments.

The menu offers waffles, crème brûlée, apple tart, banana and chocolate tart, brioche, seasonal fruit tarts, ice creams, apple crumble, and cakes. The teas are loose leaf and prepared in metal infusers in porcelain teapots. A little dish is delivered to the table for the infuser once the tea has brewed. Teas include Earl Grey with flower petals, Gunpowder green, Darjeeling, Ceylon Kenilworth, Strong Breakfast blend, Assam, Lapsang Souchong, Brunch tea (a blend of Darjeeling and Assam), Caravan Superior, Keemun, Sichuan, Caramel, and Tropical.

• Tea room open Tues.-Sat. noon–10:30pm, Sun. noon-8pm. Closed Monday. • Nearest station: Versailles main station • Tel: 01 39 50 76 44 • Major credit cards • Teas and savory and sweet dishes à la carte • E

Shopping Sites for Tea Lovers

La Route du Thé
26 rue de Satory, Versailles, 78000

If you visit Versailles by train, instead of turning right out of the station towards the château, turn left and wander down through the old Saint-Louis district of the town. Enjoy the fascinating narrow streets and squares, churches, bars, restaurants, and smart shops selling antiques, decorative objects, and interior decoration services. Here you will find this lovely shop owned and run by the delightful Elizabeth Toulooh, who is helped on weekends by her husband Hadi.

A large statue of Buddha watches over the shop, shedding a sense of calm and drawing you in. Elizabeth smiles her warm welcome and offers you a bowl of tea, inviting you to look around. The shop is stylish, classy, and intriguing. It holds a wonderful mixture of fascinating tea things – a vast selection of excellent world teas, tea bowls and pots from all over the world, jams and jellies, antique Chinese porcelains and furniture, and rugs and other treasures from the Orient.

Elizabeth and Hadi have created an enticing adventure that is irresistible. You'll be tempted with fabulous teas, gentle kindness and a magical selection of beautiful gifts.

Versailles is a quick and easy train ride from Paris. Allow no less than three hours to visit Château Versailles. The entrance queue can become quite long at mid-day. Ticket prices drop each afternoon at 3:30pm and, best of all, there is no admission fee during the week for walking the incredible palace gardens, which remain open for strolling until sunset.

Tea retail store selling hundreds of top quality world teas, open Tues.-Sat. 10:30am-7pm • Nearest station: Versailles main station • Tel: 01 39 53 12 07 • Major credit cards • laroutedthe@ wanadoo.fr • www.rout-eduthe.com • Vast selection of teas from all over the world including Laos, Vietnam, Brazil, puerhs, compressed teas, jams, jellies, teapots, bowls, antiques, rugs, caddies, and more.

Tea in the City: Paris
An index to sipping and shopping

Alphabetical list of tea rooms and lounges

Shopping Sites for Tea Lovers

Kusmi Tea (6e) 58
Lafayette Gourmet (9e) 92
Lafayette Maison (9e) 92
Lyne's (6e) 59

Old England – Fortnum & Mason (9e) 92

Le Palais des Thés (3e) 34
Le Palais des Thés (6e) 60
Le Palais des Thés (6e) (a separate company) 61
Le Palais des Thés (16e) 100
Le Palais des Thés (14e) 100

Le Parti du Thé (11e) 93

La Route du Thé (5e) 39
La Route du Thé (5e) 40
La Route du Thé (15e) 101
La Route du Thé (Versailles) 113

Terre de Chine (4e) 35
Les Thés d'Emilie-Twinings (8e) 80
Thés Emmanuel Laffarge (14e) 103
Thé ô Dor (16e) 102

Additional photos courtesy of Ladurée (p15), Hôtel Ritz Paris (p20), Park Hyatt (p23), Le Palais des Thés (p34), Dalloyau Luxembourg (p47), Delicabar (p48), Emporio Armani Café (p49), Ladurée (p50), Dalloyau Faubourg (p63), Hôtel Plaza Athénée (p64), Hôtel Le Bristol (p65-66), Hôtel George V (p67), Hôtel de Crillon (p74), and Le Palais des Thés (p100-101).

National Holidays in France

The following days and events typically are national holidays, though the exact list varies from year to year.
If no exact day is listed, the date may vary.
New Year's Day (Jan. 1)
Epiphany (Jan. 6)
Easter Sunday
Labor Day (May)
V-E Day (May)
Ascension Sunday
Pentecost
Bastille Day (July 14)
Assumption of Mary
All Saints' Day (Nov. 1)
Armistice Day (Nov. 11)
Christmas (Dec. 25)

Also available from Benjamin Press:

Tea in the City: New York
Tea in the City: London
The Great Tea Rooms of Britain
The Great Tea Rooms of America
The New Tea Companion
Looking Deeply into Tea

www.benjaminpress.com

JANE PETTIGREW
Author

Jane Pettigrew gained immediate respect as an author and tea expert when her first book, *Jane Pettigrew's Tea-Time*, was published in England. The book was subsequently translated into French, German, Italian, and Finnish, and Jane followed it with nineteen other volumes on topics related to tea, food, and etiquette. Her definitive book on the history of tea in England, *A Social History of Tea*, was published by the National Trust of England. She also served as editor of the journal, *Tea International*, and has lectured about tea throughout Europe, Asia and the Americas.

A former tea room proprietor (Tea-Time in Clapham, England), Jane still revels in the pleasure of taking tea with old friends or convincing new acquaintances of the wonders of her favorite beverage.

BRUCE RICHARDSON
Series Producer and Photographer

Bruce Richardson spends much of his time educating Americans in the art of celebrating afternoon tea. As a writer, photographer, tea blender, and frequent guest speaker at tea events across the nation, he draws from his fourteen years of experience operating one of America's best-known tea rooms – the Elmwood Inn in Perryville, Kentucky.

Bruce is the author of ten books on tea, including *The Great Tea Rooms of Britain* and *The Great Tea Rooms of America*. He and Jane Pettigrew co-authored *The New Tea Companion* for the National Trust of England in 2005. He is a columnist for *Fresh Cup* magazine and a contributing writer to several tea-related publications. Bruce and his wife, Shelley, are the owners of Elmwood Inn Fine Teas and Benjamin Press.

Benjamin Press
Publisher: Shelley Richardson
Managing Editor: Freear Williams
Senior Project Editor: Patsi Trollinger

Other books in this series:
Tea in the City: New York
Tea in the City: London

Order online at www.benjaminpress.com